AF270596

three six five

prompts, acts, divinations

an inexhaustible compendium
for writing

three
six
five

prompts, acts,
divinations

an inexhaustible
compendium
for writing

by lucy ives

with drawings
by nick mauss

siglio 2026

Book and cover design: Natalie Kraft
First printing | ISBN: 978-1-938221-37-8
Printed and bound by Artron in China

siglio uncommon books at the intersection of art & literature
po box 234, south egremont, massachusetts 01258
www.sigliopress.com t: 310-857-6935

Available to the trade through D.A.P./Artbook.com
75 Broad Street, Suite 630, New York, NY 10004
t: 212-627-1999   f: 212-627-9484

table of contents

why I wrote—and how to use—this book

Since we're speaking of serious time here, a year, I'll begin with a mildly embarrassing anecdote. To break the ice.

Once upon a time, I thought I was a machine for writing.

Laugh if you want, but it's true. This wasn't something you could see with bare eyes, and I would never have shared this predilection with you, even if you'd asked me. What machine-like qualities did I possess? I'm not sure if I came equipped with a QWERTY keyboard or character-space-endowed display, but I was for sure an item of technology, my sole setting: *Graphomania!!* I was an early means of inscription on certain days, if you can believe it—a mere stylus or twig trailing water on hot rock. I was process. I was the dream of an alphabet. I generated difference.

Imagining I was a machine for writing felt good. That's why I did it. It felt like a relief or fun mental game. I engaged in the fantasy nonstop. Being a machine for writing spared me the necessity of being a person, which was an activity that felt not good, nor easy, nor, moreover, possible. "Being a person is a specific kind of art," I wrote in a poem when I was twenty-five. This was not an art I liked to practice.

Personness was, in fact, agony. It was a condition I experienced, at a fundamental level, as a form of disenfranchisement. I tried to convince myself that it might nevertheless be a project with a method. As a machine for writing, perhaps I could become acquainted with that method and live life somewhat successfully. Perhaps I'd be able to pass as human by camouflaging my mechanistic activities as art.

Fast-forward to the present: I'm not a machine anymore and I wasn't one then, when I fantasized about it. Today I'm mostly a skeptic—who has recently retired her smartphone. I am interested in philosophy, poetics (which is to say, *making*, broadly defined), and reduction of harm (a phrase I'm also using in a broad way). Maybe the third item on this list goes without saying or isn't supposed to be said. Certainly, it's far from clear that writing itself is fundamentally liberating or kind. The contemporary era is beset with forces who want to convince us that language can be lossless-ly quantified and, meanwhile, that the end user's desire is a semi-agricultural product to be relentlessly harvested, free to the taker. I have no doubt that some of the most insidious voices among this crowd are folks who once wanted to write a "great novel." But given that novels require vulnerability as well as certain kinds of ethical reckoning, they do this instead. They push us toward their post-literate utopia.

I understand their jealousy, if not their conclusions. As a former machine, I can relate. Not having a point of view is an extremely curious thing, although it's something we speak about casually all the time. Not having a point of view is a form of forgetting *you must learn*. Someone must teach it to you, or you must acquire it: from a family, school, nation, boss, and so on. It isn't a default. Oh, and one of the other things you must learn is to forget that you forgot—and then to forget that you forgot that you forgot. Ad infinitum. The work is never complete. This is why there are so many movies about the failure of implanted memory; one can never fully close that door.

Q. *So what kind of memory are you interested in, Lucy?*

A. *The kind of memory in which forgetting is permitted.* Forgetting hasn't been sundered from this memory. They live together, messy and contentious roommates. This is not the instrumentalized memory of data-become-information, nor is it idealized memory of the sort

Socrates, Plato, & Co. tore their beards out about and insisted everyone sublimate toward. This is something more fallen and frighteningly available. It already belongs to you. You have endless amounts. You can never run out. You're human.

I really believe that writing is related to survival and, more specifically, to the survival of intuition. This is the survival of that which cannot be fully assimilated—as information or truth. Intuition is, additionally, a human thing that is not scarce and cannot become scarce, even amid the most tyrannical austerities. Intuition is previous to institutional forms. It's occult, which is to say, a recessive feature of human agency. Its exercise is not direct. It entails guessing, faith, risk, patience, cunning, awe, doubt, trust, hope, mystification, uncertainty, acceptance, and occasionally doing nothing at all (among other modalities). You have not forgotten intuition, although you may have learned that you did. Please find in this book some suggestions for how to unlearn this forgetting, should that be your wish.

I would also like to note that I take an interest in attitudes of kindness toward that which we find unbearable, particularly regarding ourselves. That the unbearable can become a gift, a material, a something that does not need to be discarded or turned away from in horror, seems significant to me. We need an illogical substance in this turning/task, something I might call "recalcitrant gentleness." In daring to apply this sort of orientation to our own histories and those of others, we have need of revised forms of realism and representation. We must make writing more prismatic and multisensory, combinatory and irreducible, porous and deep, vibratory and timely, young and old, all at once. The hope is to train an inner ear that isn't an ear, per se. This is an "ear" that hears paradox.

A last layer. Given that we are talking about writing, we will inevitably be talking about sense and semantics. We will be talking about meaning and intention. All the same, much will be left to chance. Much will remain available to interpretation. Much will be nonsense. Fate and will are but periodically synchronous—which is not nothing. And yet. Often the task is not to know what we mean, but to be in the right place at the right time. The task is to be open to what we do not expect, haven't expected, didn't know we could or were allowed to expect. If you can do that for art, surely you can do it elsewhere.

Other than the time and energy necessary for responding to these prompts, which are non-negligible goods, all the exercises in this book are meant to be done using stuff you already own. You will usually need a writing implement and a surface to write on, but you could do a lot of this in your head. I acknowledge the existence of smartphones, personal computers, and other popular gear and their affordances in a small number of exercises—feel free, of course, to skip or modify these if you find such suggestions intrusive. In essence, these proposals are designed to be attempted in brief spans of time, fragments even, dribs and drabs. You need not reorganize your life or purchase anything to do them, and many will involve strengthening relationships with people around you, as well as refamiliarizing yourself with your home and the broader ecosystem you inhabit.

This said, these prompts won't solve all your problems or even any of your problems. They might make something happen. If you are inclined to be a witness to that something and that happening, chances are, something will happen after that. Surprise will be on offer. Surprise at oneself is an aspect of human experience not lacking in beauty, or so I believe.

As a final flourish, I want to indicate that this book began with an exercise I call "Exercise for Writing from Memory." You'll find it collected here as no. 72, if you'd like to flip to it now. I may have composed this exercise spontaneously (a thing I sometimes do) during a class I was teaching in the fall of 2014, a little more than a decade ago. I'm not sure. I do know that there were about twenty people who inspired this exercise and that I continued to offer it to others, long after the grades were turned in and we all went home for break. The exercise may have mutated or molted before I finally wrote it down for the first time, which was probably in 2018 or so. Again, I'm not sure. That people liked this exercise was great, but what I've appreciated far more is their (your) willingness to participate—to experience the experiment, particularly given that some of the requests the exercise makes are impossible to fulfill (or seem that way). Thank you, acquaintances and friends, for determining that, yes, it's OK to attempt impossible things. Thank you for generously risking that. And to those who are new to this material, whichever year or years you find yourself traversing as you read: Please dare.

Open the door.

—LI, January 2025

three hundred and sixty-five prompts, acts, and divinations*

*In the exercises that follow, the reader/user is often asked to contemplate and write about themselves. A note that the self or selves so implied need not be "true," actual, genuine, or autobiographical. Dream selves, provisional selves, artificial selves, (im)possible selves, improbable selves—all are welcome (and perhaps necessary).

short-term memory

no. 1

Walk to a place where you can sit awhile undisturbed.

Now write a detailed account of how you got there.

The shorter the trip, the longer the account should be.

circular novel

no. 2

Tell the story of a journey you once took to a place where you never arrived.

sky writing

no. 3

Write a story set entirely in the future tense.

survival of intuition
no. 4

Select a book. As you read, make a note of all and any questions posed in it. (I would define "question" as a sentence ending with "?" but you may certainly count other constructions as questions, if you choose.)

Gather these questions somewhere.

Use the questions to generate something new by allowing yourself to respond, at your leisure, to each of them. Permit the context of the questions to shift, so that they refer to the world you live in, rather than to the world of the book in which you found them.

under erasure

no. 5

Have a question in mind. Ask about the future or something you are having difficulty understanding.

Now find a text someone is attempting to discard. You could look in the recycling bin or find a book abandoned on a stoop.

You might xerox this item, tear out a page, etc.

Use a pen or something else to cross letters and words out, until new sense emerges, perhaps in response to your original question or to another question, as you continue to bear your first question in mind.

neighbor

no. 6

Ask a stranger, acquaintance, neighbor, or other community member for a topic for a piece of writing.

Commit to writing about whatever they suggest in advance of the request.

life writing

no. 7

Compose a piece that is somehow a collaboration with an animal, preferably non-domesticated. How you define this collaboration is up to you (and, of course, the animal).

Microscopic beings welcome.

room for speculation
no. 8

Create an imaginary gallery or waiting area that contains images of, or figures associated with, a future (or futures) that never came to pass: your future, collective future(s), future(s) of an invented character or world.

When you leave this imaginary room, what sort of threshold must you cross? Describe this threshold.

Use what you discover here as the basis for another piece of writing.

room language

no. 9

Rearrange a room before writing. Move furniture, decorative objects, lighting, or books, perhaps thinking about the edges of the room, its openings (doors, windows), its center.

other calendars

no. 10

Here are two possible practices related to the calendar.

Look for a discarded calendar, maybe in a drawer at home or a second-hand store. Ideally, the calendar should be sparingly filled out, if at all. (Always entertaining to come across past attempts at organizing one's life that were subsequently abandoned.)

Now use the calendar as a notebook or "daybook" and fill it out over time. How you write in it is up to you: It could be a space to compose very short things serially. Perhaps it could be the fictional diary of somebody or somebodies; or the site of records of walks, meditations, meteorological observations, and/or other forms of contemplation.

Alternatively, find another way to mark time (non-calendar, non-clock) and continue this for some extended period. You might use materials other than language. Move an object each day. Begin to gradually turn objects in your house upside down. Draw single lines in places someone might see them (or not). Use a disposable camera to take a daily photograph at an appointed time. Collect and wash/repair items that have been discarded outdoors. Generate a collection or heap of some sort by means of a slow method. Consider it evidence.

exercise for indeterminancy
no. 11

Write a sentence that is or becomes a drawing.

If you have time, write about the space and time in which the line is neither fully language nor fully picture. Or see how long you can remain in this indeterminate zone.

impasse

no. 12

Draw a picture of a conflict or impossibility. Then write about it.

end as matrix
no. 13

I tend to ignore endings, as a writer of narrative. I get excited about the opening, when we first meet whomever and become acquainted with the conditions of the imagined world. Like when you go into a previously unknown garden and inhale the greenness and damp and sap (forgive the tortured simile!). But we all know, without even having to think about it much, that endings are full, too. They are maybe fuller than beginnings, in a certain way. This feels mysterious to me.

A suggestion: Describe in detail the ending of a story. This could be the ending of a story you didn't write. It could be a cliché. For example, "In the end, she lost everything."

(If I wrote such an ending, I'd try to figure out what each word means, particularly "lost" and "everything." I'd make a diagram, probably, showing the series of events that led to this dispossession. I'd make a catalog of the dispossession itself.)

Walk around in the ending. See it from different points of view and explore its contours and ambiguities. Stay with it for a few days.

Now you are free to begin.

reconstruction

no. 14

Begin a story with a remnant, trace, residue, scrap, fragment, hint, or clue. Rebuild from here.

how to walk backward
no. 15

Write a description of your bed after you have slept in it. Write a description of a chair after you have sat in it. Write a description of a room after you have closed the door. Write a description of an empty glass after a meal. Write a description of a person you no longer know. Write a description of a belief you no longer hold. Write a description of something that is so far out of sight it cannot be seen. Where did that last thought of yours, the one you were having just moments ago, come to an end? Turn toward the now-invisible place from whence you came. Wave slowly.

inverse relationship
no. 16

Describe a trip you take habitually, to a grocery store, to a job, to a place you get coffee or some other crucial semi-necessity, to a place you visit simply because it makes you happy, to the home of a relative or friend, and so on. This trip should be a trip that feels fundamental in some way to who you are right now and, significantly, represents a detour or inefficiency on your part, perhaps one you are just noticing now. Why, for example, do you frequent that faraway café or drive that winding road? You could also write about a trip you took habitually in the past and no longer take.

If the trip is long, write a single sentence about it.

If the trip is short, write a novel about it.

non-update

no. 17

Choose something that doesn't (seem to) change. Visit this thing or place each day for an extended period. Each time you visit, write about what you find. Be meticulous.

a void

no. 18

Tell the story of a day when you lost something, but with a twist—describe everything that took place, save for the loss and the lost item, person, etc.

counterfactuals

no. 19

Write a story that is a list of things that didn't happen. Allow these things that didn't happen to suggest, indirectly, what did.

autobiography of images
no. 20

Rewatch a movie with which you are familiar and about which you have strong feelings. Maybe it's your favorite film or one you saw for the first time at a pivotal moment. Maybe it upsets you in some way or makes you feel cozy and dreamy.

While you are watching the film, make detailed notes in which you describe, as objectively as possible, what is happening onscreen. Describe people's movements, colors and objects you see, the appearance of desire or intent, weather, food. Record things said and suspicions you feel.

Set these notes aside for a week to a year—for as long as you can bear to leave them alone. Return to them and reread them in a personal light. Next shape them into an autobiographical account, in which you describe an event or period in your own life. Try to locate yourself in what you saw on the screen and the notes you made.

Or—if all this seems impossible—write a fictional account in which you are the protagonist of events you never experienced.

a mask

no. 21

Have a character tell a story that is false, a lie. The caveat: Only you, the writer, know that the story is untrue. The character, by contrast, believes what they are saying and construes it as truth. If you like, you can have another character appear who attempts to convince the first character otherwise. Or you might permit the character to sustain the lie and see where this goes.

in memory of my feelings
no. 22

Make a personal timeline of all your life's secrets—secrets regarding yourself, especially, but also secrets you have kept for others, as well as secrets you may not have kept or had to keep, but knew about, all the same.

Date the secrets, paying particular attention to their inception and their conclusion, if such things exist.

You might also rank them by size, level of devastation, unwieldiness, deliciousness; place them in alphabetical order; index them; and so on.

Continue to work on this document until a new path becomes clear.

detective vs. spy

no. 23

A lie may be defined as something that appears but doesn't exist. A secret, on these terms, is something that exists but doesn't appear. One is visible but has no being. The other exists but can't be seen.

Using this differentiation, make two separate lists of all the lies and secrets you have encountered during your life. Pay particular attention to the appearance and nonappearance of each. Are any of the secrets and lies entwined? What kind of distance is between them?

Use your list as a basis for a narrative.

usable past, part one

no. 24

Write a fiction that masquerades as a historical document or that is written by a historian. Whether it speaks of history, as such, may be another question.

usable past, part two
no. 25

Mine your drafts (email) folder. Situations abound!

parafiction

no. 26

Write a fiction that presents itself as a genuine document and true account. Insist on its truth or, failing that, its genuineness.

screen memory

no. 27

Write about a false memory.

If you're not sure how to identify a false memory or believe you don't have any false memories, write about the problem of locating one.

eyes wide shut

no. 28

Describe a person who has taken on a false identity. Are they able to take this identity "off"?

the square root of minus one is plus or minus one

no. 29

Write a short study or story in which the narrator is unsure whom they are describing. In other words, the narrative or plot of the piece should be primarily concerned with attempting to determine whom or what the piece is about.

Define how you will carry out this task in advance. The narrator could attempt to use an objective metric to discover who is doing the things that take place or simply spend all their time dithering, in a state of confusion. The piece should end either with the narrator determining the identity of the protagonist or giving up on the task altogether.

the colonel's daughter

no. 30

Describe a character (and tell a story) only by describing someone with whom they are close. Do not describe the character in question themselves—insofar as you can avoid it.

bad time
no. 31

Write a story narrated by the protagonist's worst enemy.

eclipse

no. 32

Write one half of a dialogue between two people.

This might be a conversation, interview, or other.

Remember, write only one half of the dialogue. Leave space—visually, mentally, musically—for questions, responses, retorts we cannot perceive.

(The silent speech we do not hear and cannot read is nevertheless present and becomes a notable, maybe energetic, absence.)

immaculate corpses

no. 33

Gather accounts of others' experiences and the ways they think about human qualities, then create a single character who has all of these experiences and qualities. You might obtain this information (i.e., the experiences and qualities) by asking questions or posing prompts ("Tell me about a time when you experienced true joy," for example). You could ask people you know well, such as friends or family, or you might ask strangers to help you with this task.

Write a story about this synthetic character, even or especially if the character has qualities or interests you would not normally treat in writing.

If working in a group: Another option is to create a questionnaire about a character and fill it out together. You could pass the questionnaire around in a circle, adding qualities such as name, date of birth, place of residence, job, likes, dislikes, fears, ambitions, and so on, until the paper is complete. Everyone in the group should receive a copy, and each writes their own story about the character.

(This exercise owes a debt to Robert Glück's novel *Margery Kempe*.)

exercise for eloquence
no. 34

Write a story in which the narrator refuses to tell the story. Permit the narrator to come close to telling the story—perhaps longing to tell the story, speculating about how much fun it would be to tell the story, stumbling and almost telling the story, attempting (and failing) to speak about other things.

Have a character (or that character's relative or close friend) write a preface to the book that the character features in. Be sure to include this character's (strong) feelings about the book.

quixotic, part two
no. 36

Write about a character who invents their own readers.

exercise for generating influence
no. 37

Write a story with a narrator who is extremely intrusive—and may intervene in events.

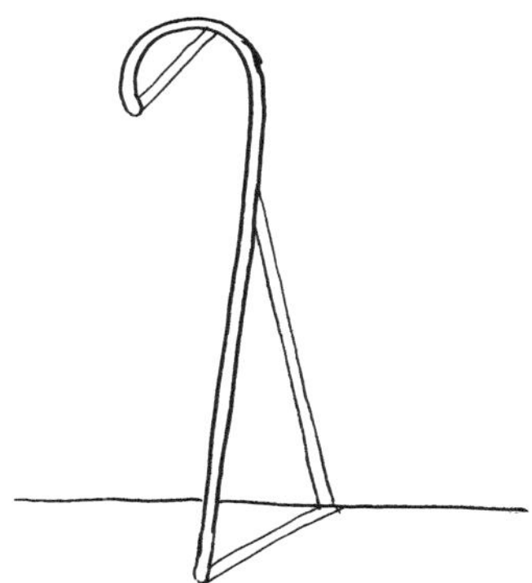

tragicomic

no. 38

Write a story about meeting yourself.

Go to a public location where you can sit relatively undisturbed and listen. Eavesdrop on a conversation near you. Make a note of what each person says, then do your best to translate what they have said into what they "really mean."

You will notice that it may take so long to write what someone "really means" that you may lose track of the conversation altogether. That's OK. Just pick up again wherever you can.

Later, perhaps when you return home, write a new dialogue.

three letters
no. 40

Write three letters:

1. A letter to a former teacher

2. A letter to a former lover

3. A letter to a current or former enemy

The further you must travel back in time to find these people, the better.

Use these letters as the basis/beginning for other writing.

memories of the future
no. 41

Although it's relatively common to hear people talk about the nonlinearity or discontinuity of present time, it is rare to set out to experience time's pertinence to forms other than the line.

This is an exercise designed to emphasize time's folded nature, its nearness to the loop and the spiral.

Choose a length of time that interests you: three weeks, six months, a year—whatever suits. This should be a length of time that allows whatever you consider meaningful change to transpire in your life, and that permits the act of forgetting to occur.

Now write a letter in which you describe in detail what is happening in this very moment. Describe where you are as you are writing, who the people you are close to in this moment are and what is occurring in your relationships with them, what you dreamed about last night, what your recent eating habits have been, what you fear right now, what you hope for, and so forth.

At the close of the letter, ask a question. The question should be about something of significance to you.

Copy the text of your letter into an email, address it to yourself, and schedule it to be sent in the length of time you specified above. (Alternatively, use print, a friend, and snail mail.)

In the future, when you receive the letter, answer the question.

missing persons

no. 42

Source a paper letter you received in the past and kept. Reread it and reflect on it. Write about its status in present time. Who were and are the sender and receiver? Do either of these people seem strange to you? Do you still understand their relationship? How have things changed?

thank-you note
no. 43

Nothing too complicated here, just a suggestion to compose a note of thanks.

OK, or with a few complications:

1. Write a letter of thanks to a (real or imagined) person who has behaved in an inconsiderate and/or selfish way—possibly toward you. See what emerges in the attempt to thank them.

2. Write a letter of thanks to a feeling, inanimate object, location, concept, time of day, or any other entity that does not usually receive such letters.

3. Write a letter of no thanks, about something that never happened to no one at no time and in no place, and your lack of gratitude and/or relief in relation to that nonevent.

Attempt to send your letter.

improved polonius
no. 44

Write a story or poem in which all language is a cliché or piece of received wisdom.

legacies

no. 45

Compile a list of things you have inherited. These could be material things, aspects of your physical form, aspects of your emotions or thoughts, a way of being in your body, names, ailments, forms of fate, secrets, etc.

Now make a list of things that you did not inherit, which is to say, things you have created yourself that are significant to who you are.

Are these two lists in dialogue? Do they overlap at all? What, in your opinion, is required to create things in a world that has been created by others? Which entries trouble you most on each of the lists?

on debt

no. 46

Make a list of all your influences. These may be personal, creative, intellectual, "negative," stylistic, other.

Write this list by hand and the more influential a given influence is, the larger or bolder you should make the letters comprising its name.

advice
no. 47

"Advice" is not usually considered a literary genre or form—but it might be. Write a piece that takes the form of advice. This advice might be overbearing, or it might be too vague, come too late, and so on. It might be unwanted. And, of course, it might be destined to be ignored.

exercise for relief
no. 48

Choose to resign from some role, position, state, whatever you like (it's not necessary that this be a job).

Write a letter of resignation.

Do not send it.

Repeat this process as needed.

hounds of love

no. 49

Write the truest story you can of a time you suffered deeply in/through a relationship with another person.

When you are done, attempt (one or more of) the following alterations:

1. Set the story in the future or the historical past, in an alternative world or another country.

2. Choose a voice, perspective, or style other than your own, e.g., horror or adventure story, newspaper article or advice column, point of view of a bystander, as told on a deathbed, etc.

3. Adjust the story's ethical or moral balance (i.e., change who is to blame and/or who has agency).

Lastly, select new names and physical descriptions to complete the alteration.

unrequited

no. 50

Write a piece in which you give someone permission not to love you.

What you do after this is up to you.

lost cause

no. 51

Create a matrix with four quadrants: *known knowns, unknown unknowns, known unknowns,* and *unknown knowns.*

These categories may be defined as follows: a *known known* is something that someone knows and is aware they know (basically, something that someone knows), an *unknown unknown* is something that someone doesn't know and isn't aware they don't know, a *known unknown* is something that someone knows they don't know, and an *unknown known* is something that someone isn't aware that they know.

Use these categories to analyze a story you have written or to parse a situation you would like to write about. Consider the *unknown known* the beginning—or end—of a new narrative.

eros

no. 52

Write one thousand words about a ten-second event that cannot change the world yet is not a repetition.

never alas

no. 53

Write a motto.

It can be provisional or impermanent. You need not live by it, but you could.

inversion

no. 54

Select a scene, perhaps a famous one, from a well-known novel. This scene should be a couple of pages long and should include at least two characters. Now invert the scene's values. What was bad in the past should become good, what is ugly should be beautiful, cruel kind, and so on. Where inversion is not possible, improvise. Edit your new text until it seems to make sense. Change all names. Retitle the piece and make it your own.

undoing

no. 55

Write a story in which everything happens in reverse.

making americans
no. 56

Locate an unassuming sentence of twenty-five words or less. See how many new sentences you can make with the words it contains by rearranging and repeating them. Make as many new sentences as you can. Attempt to write a short story using only the words included in the original sentence. Your short story must have a beginning, middle, and end, and something must change during its course.

same but different
no. 57

This task is very simple, yet it can result in lovely innovations.

Create a series of narrative vignettes in which one element remains the same while all else changes.

The "same" element might be a frame, a setting, an event, a color, the use of dates, a word count, a particular thematic approach, a gesture, a character . . .

Continue the series until a narrative either emerges—or doesn't.

bizarro
no. 58

Create an alternative universe identical to our own universe save that one thing is different.

Tell a story about what takes place there.

metempsychosis
no. 59

Write a story about a character who leaves a place that is familiar to them to go to a place that is unfamiliar or perhaps unrecognizable.

As part of this journey, the character's body must change in some way.

werewolf

no. 60

Write from the point of view of a nonhuman animal. Question and contemplate narrative, the senses as we know them through language, language itself, linear time, reason, spatial logics, dreams, desire, psychology, human violence.

Rewrite a well-known fairy tale.

Should you so choose, attempt the following adjustments:

1. Insert a contemporary detail.

2. Enact a reversal: A villain is good, the hero evil. Or invert another hierarchy or binary.

3. Treat the narrator as a character capable of intervening in events.

more inversions

no. 62

Begin a story by attempting one or both of the following:

1. Have space play the role normally assumed by *time*, and vice versa.

2. Set the story in an ostensibly insignificant or impossible location, such as the inside of an air-conditioning unit or the dip in a spoon.

perforations

no. 63

This is a thought for notetaking. It is additionally a way to check in on the multiplicity of times we inhabit, even without our full recognition of these times/habitations.

Carry a small notebook with you one day wherever you go. Whenever you find yourself thinking of the past, write down the year/date/time of day (or anything you can piece together to approximately index this), along with the time when you had this thought.

For example, "July 20-something, 2023, afternoon, X poses near statue — 11:12 a.m."

Keep the practice going for at least twelve hours.

See what emerges.

telegraph

no. 64

Sit somewhere where you are unlikely to be disturbed. Close your eyes (or leave them open) and imagine that you can expand your sensory consciousness so that you can touch the walls of the room you are seated in. Next, attempt to widen your awareness so that it moves beyond the walls to the outdoors. Continue to expand. Periodically write down the thoughts that come into your mind as you engage in this exercise.

in praise of shadows
no. 65

Locate the shadows nearest you.

Describe them. What are their qualities? Which colors do they contain? Do they return, day in and day out? What significance do they hold for you? What do these shadows hide or reveal? What is inside them?

the character
no. 66

This is an exercise for developing new work, possibly in a classroom setting.

Place an empty chair at the front of a classroom—or, if you are somewhere else (such as your kitchen), find a chair and put it in a place you like.

Ask yourself/participants/students to write a piece describing someone who was sitting in the chair three years ago.

self-portrait in a convex light bulb
no. 67

Without getting up from your habitual workspace, find a reflective surface that is not, strictly speaking, a mirror. This could be the edge of a chrome lamp or coffee pot, a dark part of your computer screen, an iPhone case, an unilluminated light bulb, a glass-framed photograph hanging on the wall.

Describe the world you see in this object's surface.

taste test

no. 68

Write a detailed description of the process of drinking a glass of water, eating an apple, or the act of ingesting some other small meal. Renovate your conception of what constitutes an event.

suspended animation
no. 69

Return to a moment when you paused yesterday (to make a cup of coffee, because your car got stuck on an icy hill, while someone took a long time to finish their sentence) and describe what you thought as you waited for the next moment to come.

Can you recreate the sensation of the event taking form, particularly if the event wasn't in doubt (for example, the water was going to boil)?

threshold music

no. 70

Make a list of each thought you had as you were falling asleep last night.

dream ladder
no. 71

Make a list of all the dreams you can remember ever having dreamed.

Begin with the most recent dreams and work your way backward to the beginning of your life.

Describe each of the dreams. If there are things you can't remember, that's OK.

Now underline nouns throughout your descriptions. Underline verbs.

Make lists of: places, agents, objects, actions.

Using these lists, write a new work—a poem or narrative piece—that employs these words.

exercise for writing from memory
no. 72

This is an exercise for writing from memory with five instructions:

1. Describe your earliest memory.

2. Describe something that happened yesterday.

3. Describe something that happened a week ago yesterday.

4. Describe something that happened five years ago yesterday.

5. Describe something you have completely forgotten.

A note about the spirit in which you may wish to respond to the five instructions: If you don't quite recall something, that's just fine. Stick with that feeling rather than reaching for fact. Linger with each instruction (say, for a page or more). You may discover something unexpected. If you are asking, "But how can I describe something I've completely forgotten?!" you are on the right track.

history of styles
no. 73

Write the history of a style.

Identify a style whether old or new (Victoriana, '90s minimalism, Memphis, etc.).

Make lists of attributes, examples, areas of absolute rejection, aspirations, narratives, politics, and so on, associated with this style.

Locate the style's inception, if possible, and predict its future. What are the drawbacks of this style? What are its insights? Does this style hide or run rampant? Does it possess its own uncanny agency? Is it immortal? Does it have siblings?

Alternatively, replace the term *style* with *custom, convention,* or *system.*

delectation

no. 74

Write an essay about a particular taste (define this noun as you prefer).

Offer an anatomy of this taste, its meanings, its various appearances, its history.

parasocial

no. 75

Write a short story (or poem) in which all the characters are living celebrities. It doesn't matter if they know one another in real life or do things that celebrities would or can do. In fact, it's better if they don't—or, if they do, they might say things that are "out of character" and move through unexpected scenes and landscapes. Include politicians and successful visual artists, if of interest.

lore

no. 76

On your own—or, working with others, inside or outside a class—
gather local legends and myths, beliefs about charms, examples of
coincidence and the uncanny, authorless songs, rhymes recited for
fun or for ritual purposes, rituals, spells, notions about supernatural
possibilities, hauntings, and games you learned and participated in
as a child. Make an encyclopedia of these practices and orientations.
Write something based on what you learn and what this research
allows you to imagine.

gardening at night
no. 77

Research your own family tree. Identify at least three ancestral "land-ing sites" back in time beyond your parents. (For me, this would entail attempting to learn who my great-great-grandparents were, informa-tion I don't currently have and will have difficulty uncovering.)

Include historical events, particularly if these affect the tree or make it impossible to go further back in time or know things. What can't you know and why?

If and when possible and appropriate, ask questions of the living. Poke around in the library and online.

Write about what you learn.

time's arrow, part one
no. 78

Write about an experience you've had of a disturbance or transformation of time itself, whether the slowing of time, its speeding
up, its reordering. What caused the change? Did the change affect
sensation or consciousness? Did time eventually normalize? How and
why?

time's arrow, part two
no. 79

Write about an event in such a way that time changes pace, order, or direction, or so that the event is seen through a lens that transforms time in some way.

exercise for generation of paradox
no. 80

Write a story or vignette about the emotional life of a time traveler who has begun to regret their (temporal) mobility.

shared timeline
no. 81

Fold a sheet of paper in half.

On the left-hand side, create a personal chronology. Begin at the beginning of your life and list the most important (personal) events, culminating with the present. Do your best to remember dates and order, but don't fact-check yourself; this is meant to be a rough draft.

Now go through and add historical events on the right-hand side. Should historical events that precede your birth be included here? Again, do not verify specifics of these events; do your best to work from your conceptions without external sources of memory.

When you are done, show this timeline to someone and discuss it. Check order and dates and make any necessary corrections.

Now create another piece of writing informed by this chronology.

(This exercise was inspired by a prompt created by artist Paul Thek for his students.)

nesting

no. 82

Progress by means of inset narratives: Allow one scene or setting to contain another, and then another, and another, for as long as this seems feasible.

Journey inward, toward new exteriors.

reconciliation of monuments
no. 83

Locate all the monuments in the area where you live, or, if you reside in a large city, in a more circumscribed area such as a park or neighborhood. Make what is, to the best of your ability, a definitive list. Visit the monuments and note what they commemorate. If they commemorate events, list the events. If they commemorate people, list the people. If they commemorate something else, list that.

Compare what you have listed during your in-person visits to a local history. Are there *un*commemorated events, persons? Conversely, is there a monument that is present but has yet to be identified?

the curtain is part of the show

no. 84

Write about a *mediated* experience of a historical event. Choose an event within the ken of your own experience, even if the experience was indirect; this event may or may not have occurred during your lifetime.

archaeology of events
no. 85

Create a timeline of a character's life. You can structure this timeline using dates or major events and so on.

Now close your eyes and use your finger to point to some part of the timeline. Note where your finger has fallen and repeat this process two more times.

Take the three moments you selected and write a detailed scene for each.

When you are done, put the three scenes together, but not in chrono-logical order.

See what results from this process. Have you excavated or intuited elements of plot? Have you written a story?

nonevents

no. 86

This is an exercise for sneaking up on and exploring the nature of
narrative events. You'll need a current—or not current, it's not totally
crucial—newspaper or magazine. Print is best. You'll be looking for
something apparently unimportant in it.

Examine an article in which something takes place. Look for a detail
related to an action or activity that is tangential to whatever is treated
as significant in the prose. NB: This will not be easy.

For example, on page A11 of *The New York Times* of Friday, January 5,
2024, I see sentences such as: "Ms. Cox bought her son a version of
a Nintendo console called a RetroN, which used the same hardware
as the original Nintendo console, from a pawnshop, as well as an old
cathode-ray tube television to help him get started" and "'I'm looking
at a couple perched on the roof of the park bathroom and a couple in
a tree fort right now.'"

Find moments of stillness within such descriptions, moments direct-
ed away from the underlined events at hand, as well as unarticulated
perspectives and subjectivities. Who is present in these moments?
What do they know? What don't they know? What do they believe the
future holds? What would they say if asked to describe the past? How
do their stories differ from the one ostensibly offered to the reader?

Write a new narrative or other piece based on what you find.

# of light and folds

no. 87

Create a leporello or accordion book. Experiment with the spaces its folded (rather than bound) structure allows you to write and/or draw in. Display it on a shelf or carry it in your pocket. Keep it near you at all times, then give it away.

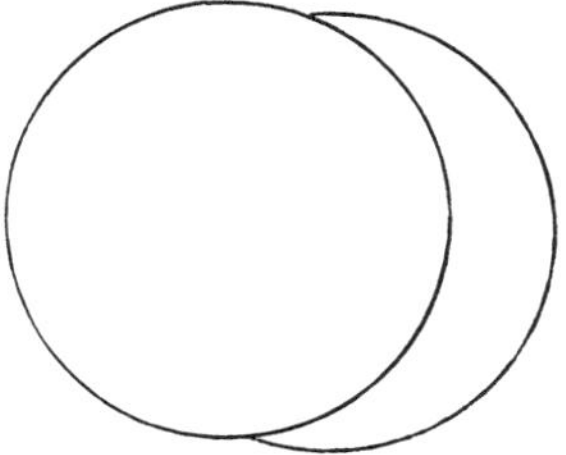

phenomenology of reading
no. 88

Write about reading as a physical, material, mental, and personal act. Describe what happens during your reading. Stray from questions of literary meaning, per se. How do memory and longing participate? How about the temperature of the air? What occurs within your body?

Chronicle the physicality of the act, as well as the qualities of time(s) generated.

dear reader

no. 89

Write a letter to the reader. Try to find out who they are.

two transcripts
no. 90

This exercise shines light on the ways in which point of view inexorably shapes our writing, as well as how attempts to "be objective" can produce unusual and very subjective results.

Go to a public place where you can sit for a little while relatively undisturbed. Bring a writing implement and something to write on.

Time yourself for five minutes and write down only what you can see transpiring before your eyes, what you can hear, etc. Aim for pure description devoid of opinions and thoughts.

Subsequently, time yourself for five minutes and write down only what you think. Try not to describe anything you see or hear around you. It's OK if you aren't writing full sentences.

Compare your two transcripts.

What would happen were you to repeat one or both procedures for twenty minutes? For an hour?

the sentence is present
no. 91

This is an exercise for finding lost or neglected experience that may be very near at hand. It takes hold of the present and cracks it open like a geode. If you don't believe me, try it.

Set a timer for ten minutes.

Now respond to each prompt below in two-minute intervals, writing with as much detail as you can:

> 5 minutes ago, I was thinking . . .

> 4 minutes ago, I was thinking . . .

> 2 minutes ago, I was thinking . . .

> 1 minute ago, I was thinking . . .

> 5 seconds ago, I was thinking . . .

music for sentences
no. 92

Begin with a sentence, perhaps an overtly general one. "Once there was ...," "Everyone knows that ...," "Above all, it is important to ...."

Select or compose a sentence of this nature that interests you and then bear it in mind.

Now select a piece of music without words.

Arrange things so that you can sit and listen to this piece of music uninterrupted for its duration.

Beginning with the sentence you chose in the first step, write while listening along to the piece of music a second time.

Follow the music's lead. Try to anticipate the ending of the piece, so that your writing concludes at the same time as the musical composition does. Simultaneously, allow yourself to wander and get lost as the song plays.

When you are finished, listen to the piece of music a third time while doing nothing.

time's signature
no. 93

Borrow a metronome and make use of it while writing.

unexhausted time

no. 94

Make a list of three new things that have transpired, or that you have
encountered, in the past month.

Now make a list of three new things that have transpired, or that you
have encountered, in the past week.

Now make a list of three new things that have transpired, or that you
have encountered, in the past two days.

Now make a list of three new things that have transpired, or that you
have encountered, in the past hour.

Now make a list of three new things that have transpired, or that you
have encountered, in the past minute.

Now make a list of three new things that have transpired, or that you
have encountered, in the past five seconds.

sabbatical
no. 95

Spend a day not speaking—or a longer time.

Document what takes place.

exercise for forgetting
no. 96

Identify something you *don't* remember about the changing of the year last year—what you ate, who you were with, what happened at the stroke of midnight, etc. Spend some time attempting to describe this ellipsis.

Now use this ellipsis to locate others. You could make a list of things or moments you don't remember and/or see how close you can come to remembering them. What takes the place of forgotten things if you can't find your way to remembering them?

These steps will surely form a basis for more writing.

gleanings
no. 97

Create a list of very briefly noted discoveries.

Possible topics for such a list:

— List of words you did not know and found while reading
  (plus definitions)

— Partially read books

— Moments of déjà vu

— Gross feelings

— Dreams about friends

Keep the list for an extended period. Let it become a companion to and
record of your life.

vividness book
no. 98

Keep a notebook in which you record examples of vivid description you find in the writings of others.

Maintain this notebook for several (many) years—until it is either full or you can no longer find writing that strikes you as more vivid than your own, whichever happens first.

reductive diary

no. 99

Choose a low number (under ten) that you like and keep a diary for a year in which you write entries with only that number of words.

If you choose five words, you can write, "We are going to laugh," for one day's entry, for example. If three words, "I enjoyed cheese," and so on. (OK, because I think it's funny, I'll go on. Two words: "Enjoyed cheese." One word: "Cheese.")

In theory, this diary could be something you compose in your head during the day and commit to a document when you have a spare twenty seconds. I find it interesting how a very short string of words like this may occupy and encode time (or not) and how one must engage memory in a particular fashion to accomplish this (extremely) minor (but potentially quite large/expansive) writing task.

daily double
no. 100

With a friend, cowrite a daily piece. Set the word count, subject(s), and terms of daily collaboration in advance.

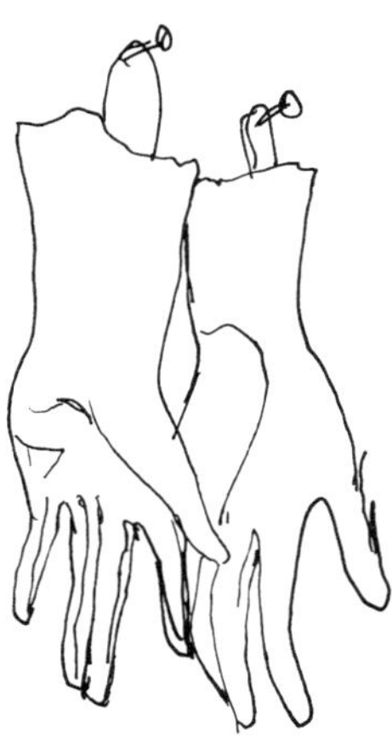

exercise for generation of names
no. 101

Identify something in the world or in history that has no name. (If you aren't sure how to identify such a thing, use your intuition and body.)

This might be an unrecognized color or shape, a concept, a human custom, an emotion, an action or gesture, a time of day, and so on.

Create a dictionary-style definition for this word/name, including etymology and perhaps other elements of provenance/word history (look at *Oxford* et al. for examples of information given).

Share this word/name, try to get others to use it, write another work about it, send it to someone in the mail.

killing a word
no. 102

Although the title of this exercise sounds a bit violent, it is in fact a contemplative undertaking. If one repeats a word for an extended duration, its meaning may die. Perhaps you've experienced this unexpectedly (it's called "semantic satiation").

Make an experiment of it: Over the course of a day, repeat a word over and over until it stops making sense. Type it twenty-five times. Write a poem in which you cause one or more words to die through incessant repetition. See what sort of effect this creates. Some words die hard (*promiscuous*, for example); some rather easily (try *new*).

What's left once a word has died? What is that strange sound, that stub, that deflated container? A poem that is the occasion of the death of a word might be something like an anatomy of that word—or, perhaps, an elegy.

This exercise can be the basis for many kinds of writing.

intricacy

no. 103

Let's focus on description for a moment.

We might think of written description as the suppression of distance, since it brings that which is not present nearer.

A suggestion: Write a very short story that takes place inside an image on a postcard.

signs of life
no. 104

This is an exercise about perception, or maybe it's a type of visual research.

Find a time when you will be a passenger in a moving vehicle (car, bus, train, etc.) for an extended period and bring along your preferred writing implement(s).

Position yourself beside a window.

During your trip, observe the landscape and the ways in which it has been altered by humans. Your task is to take notes on these alterations.

This means a bridge is no longer "a bridge." It is a particular transformation of space. Make note of the materials, forms, styles, colors, feelings, and so forth inherent to this transformation.

Do this for anything you see.

Note also transformations that have been enacted by individuals at a smaller scale: writing on walls and other surfaces, murals, discarded objects, material jokes made by passersby, carvings, attempts at gardening and other kinds of cultivation, decorations, handmade signs, piles of stuff, small monuments, shelters, paths, and other unclassifiable changes to structures and the landscape.

When you return home, make a new piece of writing based on these notes.

Repeat the process. Continue the exercise for many years.

on mending

no. 105

Keep a diary of repair.

First you will need to identify something in need of repair.

Next use the diary to chronicle the repair.

Keep the diary until it's no longer needed.

Accept that the diary may always be needed.

Attempt to rejoice in your new companion, the diary of repair.

(This exercise owes a debt to the artist Iman Mersal.)

everybody's archive
no. 106

Set aside a time at which everyone in a group may meet and share something that in some way functions as an archive for them: an object or set of objects, a collection of media (print, electronic, etc.), a website or account, memory recorded in sound, image, or text. Each person presents their archive verbally and visually, and perhaps in other ways, for around seven to ten minutes. Afterward they respond to questions from the group about the archive.

This exercise may be associated with writing, or it may be associated with something else. It tends to result in unexpected forms of information and experience: vicarious, virtual, personal, and otherwise.

ad hoc

no. 107

Assemble a notebook using only found paper. If you have access to recycling bins, this should be a (relative) snap.

Use the notebook you have created only to write down or record unoriginal content: things you didn't write (from others' books or other sources), clichés, language you discover in your environment but did not create yourself. Attempt to use the notebook and/or similar notebooks for an extended period, such as a season, semester, year, or years.

someone else's book
no. 108

Here is a relatively simple way to begin writing—particularly at a time of fatigue:

1. Select a book by another author and begin retyping/copying it. (It can be pleasurable to use a typewriter. A computer or longhand work, as well.)

2. Continue until you have fully assumed the other person's style. Or you find you must break free from it.

mysteries of scale
no. 109

This is an exercise designed to encourage the rethinking of relationships of time and narrative—and, above all, how events occur in
writing.

Try one or more of the following:

1. Compose a novel that takes place over the course of three
    sentences. The plot must begin, unfold, and end.

2. Compose a three-page novel. All actions and events must be
    represented in this space, and your three-page novel should
    have at least one hallmark of a more "standard" novel:
    revelation, reversal of fortune, love and loss, adventure,
    dissolution of the self, villainy, redemption, transformation,
    and so on.

3. Write a two-page sentence. If possible, this sentence should
    not tell a story but instead should have all the features of a
    single sentence (i.e., the sentence as a contingent entity—it
    plays a role and makes no attempt to say everything that
    might be said).

Try inventing other possibly inappropriate or risky pairings of quan-
tity of writing and form.

Enjoy.

time farm
no. 110

Use space to map time.

Plan a walk in a location you know well.

Situate, imaginatively/conceptually, points in time *in a narrative* at various sites along your walk. Then, go on the walk and visit these sites.

Take notes.

Use this method as a technique for traveling through time—whether to your past or future, or to someone else's. Let it be a tool for generating fiction.

<h1 style="text-align:center">on the museum's ruins</h1>
no. 111

When I was a teenager, I went to museums and galleries after school on Fridays and made pencil sketches of works of art (I had seen people do this in movies set in the nineteenth century). After a while, I stopped making these line drawings and started using words to reproduce paintings and other things. (Strangers commented on my early sketches, not always kindly. Words are easier to hide.)

It interested me that during these exercises I would inevitably stop writing about the work of art and start writing about something else. I became obsessed with this moment of transition.

Here are two prompts for repurposing the space of the museum.

1. Museum-as-clock: Someone recently told me a story about an individual they know who goes to visit the same work of art at the same museum at the same time on the same day every week. This person has done this every week for more than a decade. Straightforward and yet somehow terrifying! I imagine this practice holds a few possibilities for writing, including writing a single episodic, diaristic, or epistolary book that will only be completed at the end of one's life. Or maybe a year of visits would be enough. Or a month.

2. Add an object to the museum.

image as event
no. 112

If you've ever had the experience of finding a picture in the (real) world of an imagined or dreamed-about event, this exercise may make some sense to you.

This may be an exercise for revision, or it may be something else.

Go to a library or bookshelf containing art books or maybe a museum or gallery. Have in mind an imaginative work or world about which you have some curiosity (maybe it's a novel you're working on, for example).

Attempt to locate an image that depicts ("depicts") a scene from the work or world. Don't worry if all the details aren't exact; that's not the point. (Readers of tarot may be familiar with a version of this style of gaze.)

Look into the image. Investigate what is present. Permit new events, qualities, effects, and details to unfold and, meanwhile, write down what you see.

planned coincidence
no. 113

Restage and rephotograph a photograph from the past that is meaningful to you.

This should be an image that includes you—as a child, as a younger person, as a previous version of yourself.

Ask other people to help you, if it's a group photo. Props and costumes are not strictly necessary, nor does the setting need to be the same.

Caption the photo.

Now use the new image and its caption to generate a narrative or a theory—about yourself and/or your history, about your community, about photography, about the past, or about something else entirely.

in the name of a rose
no. 114

Tell a story about your name.

How you define this task is up to you.

commonplace book
no. 115

Embark on a self-archiving project.

Gather digital documents and traces of yourself. Collect messages (texts, emails, DMs), notes, logs, social media remnants, and other vestiges into a single document. Organize it, if you like.

Use a print-on-demand service to cause the document to return to you as a book. Repeat as needed.

memory palace
no. 116

The *memory palace* is an ancient technique for enhancing memory that involves imaginative "placement" of information or words to be recollected in specific locations in a remembered version of a familiar place. This exercise makes use of some of the technique's principles.

Go somewhere architecture can be found. Spend time in this location, examining what's present. Select a few locations in the place—from four to seven or so—that can become receptacles for your memories. Accord a memory to each of the locations you have chosen and make notes about the process, the place, and which memories of yours now reside there.

After you leave, compose a piece about the space. It should not be about the space you came to before you placed your memories in it, or the space or structure of your memories, themselves; rather, devise something (different) that might be constructed of both elements.

Use this writing as a setting for another work of fiction.

taste as time

no. 117

Prepare a meal from the past, perhaps a meal you shared on a special occasion or one that was habitual. If you like, treat this endeavor as a ritual.

While consuming this meal, write down what comes to mind.

your book

no. 118

Someone once asked me, "What is your book?"

They didn't want to know the title of my favorite book or the best book I had ever read. They were asking me about a book that was very meaningful to me as a kid—possibly a minor book.

I won't tell you what I said, but I will say that this conversation took place twenty-four years ago. I still remember my friend's question.

A suggestion:

Reread that book ("your book") that you loved most passionately as a younger person. Or one that obsessed you (perhaps not in a positive way).

This should be a book you still think about from time to time.

Write an essay about the book.

Take the book seriously, if you can.

Allow the essay to simultaneously serve as a work of autofiction or autotheory.

Alternatively, rewrite the book in your own words.

dress to impress
no. 119

Recall a garment you no longer possess that holds a significant place in your memory.

This might be:

- An item you gave away prematurely or lost (and were unable to recover)

- Something that did not look the way you hoped it would

- Something you wore so often it fused with your body or self

- Something you claimed from someone else's wardrobe

- Something you wore to try to send a message to someone you loved

And so on.

Describe this garment in detail.

Tell a story.

bad saint
no. 120

The task: Write a critique of romantic love.

This may be a poem, essay, play, or, if you have time, novel. Be sure to include your earliest memory of learning of the concept of romantic love.

may be

no. 121

Write a narrative piece which is driven by and composed entirely of the hypothetical, the suggestion, the wish, the *if* and the *then*. Attempt to place all verbs in the subjunctive (mood).

human nature
no. 122

Identify a delusion (of grandeur, that birds aren't real, and so on).

Now create a character who possesses or otherwise has an intimate relationship with this delusion.

spider sense

no. 123

Indulge in the most luxurious paranoia and give free rein to your suspicious side. Create a detailed drawing of a social web—of personal, familial, and economic relationships (among people you know and/or people you have invented).

For the most interesting results, create the web first, then add information naming the nodes and giving other character-related data such as names and ages.

Use this web as the basis for a piece of (fictive) writing.

far feeling

no. 124

Engage in recurring acts of telepathy with a friend who lives at a distance from you, even if this distance is only another room in the same house.

At an elected time, have one person concentrate on an image or phrase and attempt to mentally project it into the mind of the other person. Let the other person simultaneously attempt to receive it and then draw or write down whatever they perceive in their mind's eye.

Keep a record of what was sent and what received. Switch roles.

hunting days
no. 125

Make an appointment with yourself. Choose a meeting location and the time you will remain in this location. Note it in your calendar, if you keep one.

At the allotted time, go to the meeting.

When you arrive, write down an explanation of why you have come to this meeting.

Continue from here.

(If you are feeling like it's time to be kind to yourself, make several such appointments.)

sounding

no. 126

Sit at your desk, a kitchen table, on a chair in your room—somewhere in the place you live or are currently staying. The main thing is that this location should be relatively quiet and possibly familiar to you, although this second stipulation is less important.

In a notebook or on a piece of paper, write by hand, attempting to systematically identify and describe all the sounds you hear.

After you identify and describe obvious sounds, such as people talking in the hallway or the settling of the refrigerator, seek other sounds below, above, and around these sounds. Try to locate sounds whose origin is unknown, as well as sounds at a distance. Are there sounds very close by that you are neglecting? Is your body making sound? Where is there silence? What are its qualities?

Continue this work of description, carefully weighing and traveling in relation to the sounds surrounding you and within you, until your writing becomes something else.

Note that this exercise can be used anytime to initiate a practice. For many years I began my daily(ish) writing in this way.

inner ear

no. 127

What is the first sound you remember hearing? What is your earliest memory of the act of hearing itself? Do you know what produced what you heard at this time? What is your earliest memory of noise?

Respond to these prompts with the awareness that you may find yourself traveling far from the body you currently inhabit.

early poem
no. 128

Describe a (mysterious) childhood belief. Take your time and try to find the limits of this belief. What properties did your body have, according to this belief? What properties did the material world have? Who or what was present that made this belief possible? Was there something to be avoided, something forbidden, something necessary to do? Were other people, characters, or animals involved?

See where this description takes you. Use it as the basis for a longer piece of writing.

deschooling

no. 129

Write a history of your interactions with schools. One way to start might be to make a list of all the schools you attended and then compose the "true motto" of each school. Whereas the school's public motto might be "Truth," its true motto might be "Might Makes Right," for example, or "We Tried." (This will be particularly interesting for early childhood education.) You could also identify moments of indoctrination, moments of inspiration, skills acquired, and so on. You might list teachers and their qualities, games played, memorable interactions, crises.

Now write three things you didn't (and couldn't) learn in school. What would a "school" for such things be like? Select one such "school" and describe it in a work of fiction. Or write an essay on your actual schooling and how it could be, should be, might have been otherwise.

toy

no. 130

Write about a toy you had as a child that took on definitively un-toy-like qualities. What sort of world did this toy project or entail? What feelings and fantasies were associated with it?

Now write a purely physical description of the toy without considering any associated storylines or meanings asserted by the toy's creator.

If you yourself created the toy, explain why you did so.

reenactment

no. 131

Find an early piece of writing, something you wrote before the age of ten or eleven, if possible. The longer and more storylike this piece, the better.

Now revise this piece, retaining character names, setting, plot, etc., with one major difference: The revision should be in the style of something you would write today, as an older person. (Employ the mode of psychological realism, for example, if that is your thing.)

Engage with the original logic of the piece, rather than trying to correct it, even as you add elements derived from your current way of understanding both the world and writing.

exponential irresolution
no. 132

Recall or identify a loose end in your life.

This could be a lost object never reclaimed, a person who disappeared or with whom you are no longer in contact, something you were supposed to do that you never did, an event that never ended, and so on.

Describe this loose end.

Rather than attempting to resolve the loose end (or retie it), return to the moment of loss and identify something fortuitous about it. Having identified this fortuitous thing, make a list of at least seven other pleasant—or, at least, not bad—things that flow from that first thing. Finally, make a list of at least seven other fortuitous things that flow from each of the seven pleasant-ish things you first identified. (If you have time and stamina, continue with multiples of seven.)

Use this tree of exponential irresolution as the basis for a poem, essay, or other piece of writing.

on landscape

no. 133

Write the story of a journey you took with someone you loved, whom you later lost or became estranged from. What rituals were part of this journey? What happened during the journey that hadn't happened before? Did you know that you would lose this person? If so, how or why? How did you (or did you not) think of the future, at this time? What role did the place you visited play in the unfolding of your relationship?

impossible archive, part one
no. 134

Attempt to make a list of everyone you've ever met.

impossible archive, part two
no. 135

Create a series in which you interview everyone you've ever met. Given this task is impossible, you might invent another way to pay homage to your list.

This is your life. And so on.

self-index
no. 136

Here is something easier said than done:

Make an exhaustive index (to start, try an alphabetical list) of all your interests. Be strict. In other words, inclusive and honest.

When you are done with your index, you can use it in a variety of ways:

> *To write a book. To shape your own research. To know yourself. To plan the future. As an album or archive. In ways I cannot imagine or foresee.*

You might consider linking the index to things you have already done or written, to events, to friends and colleagues, and so on.

An interesting challenge: Deepen your index—in other words, try not to add new items. Rather, work with what's already there.

improved inactivity
no. 137

Write an account or schedule of what for you is an "average," or perhaps "ideal," day. Include times, locations, durations, and so on.

Do you have an "average" day? What concessions to detail must you make to engage in this description? What's the difference between what you say or believe you will do and what you actually do? Do you meet your own expectations, and how do fantasy and delusion participate in your ideas about how to spend time? How do you think about daily time? Is there anything absurd about this undertaking?

Use this exercise as a jumping-off point for something else, such as wasting a few hours in a very frivolous manner or writing a reflection on time itself.

double life

no. 138

This exercise owes a major debt to Samuel R. Delany's description of his journals.

Keep a double-entry journal by drawing a line vertically or horizontally down or across the page, or don't divide it explicitly, but, in any case, use your journal for two purposes—perhaps cross-purposes.

One part of the document should describe one aspect of your experience, the other, a different aspect. These pairings might be the life of your desire as opposed to your professional life, bodily sensation as opposed to what you believe you must do, your thoughts about your birth as opposed to your thoughts about your death, and so on.

Over time, the interrelation of these two apparently opposed aspects of living may become apparent.

your philosophy
no. 139

Chart your personal philosophy in a diagram, with or without words.

Once you are satisfied with your diagram, write the philosophy out in sentences.

Revise the philosophy, in words or image.

distraction diary
no. 140

If you work at a computer, keep a running account of what you are thinking at moments when, instead of continuing a task, you turn to "frivolous" or "unnecessary" pursuits, such as digging through social media, stalking esoteric DJs, or trawling eBay. Note your thoughts and impulses at these moments. Consider allowing the notetaking to replace the original or intended activity. Remain aimless, if possible. Observe, describe; write things you didn't mean to write and think things you didn't mean to think.

constrained dream
no. 141

I sometimes use this exercise to break the ice at the beginning of a class. I invented it spontaneously one day and was astonished by how fun and revelatory it was. Here is the prompt:

Describe a dream you had last night using only three words.

The words can be any part(s) of speech, and they don't have to make sense (obviously), although of course they will make a sense of a kind.

If we're introducing ourselves, I'll ask people to say their names, then share their constrained dream. We'll hear things like, "Kangaroo, sunglasses, mom," or "Buckets, buckets, buckets," and many other permutations. I don't think it's necessary to explain that people may fictionalize or invent dreams, but it might be nice to mention this, depending.

After everyone has had a chance to share, I sometimes ask for a volunteer to go around the room and repeat everyone's name and dream. There is usually someone present who can accomplish this task—with a little help from friends.

first impressions
no. 142

Here is a truly inexhaustible resource: What we imagine about others' lives.

Bring paper and a writing implement to a public setting and begin taking notes. As you observe those around you, try to catch yourself in the act of making assumptions about others. Don't judge yourself for doing this; rather, attempt to write down an exact transcript of what you think.

Later, transcribe and edit what you have written. Now for the tricky part: Make a portrait of yourself or personal memoir using the qualities and experiences you have attributed to others.

Watch a film with the sound off.

Transcribe what you see. Even if you know the names of the characters and what is understood to be taking place, try to keep your descriptions of the action, protagonists, and scenery as neutral as possible.

"A young person stares into space in a gray room."

"A red car slows near a blue pile of rocks."

Return to this writing after some time passes. See what sorts of narrative(s) you loaned the movie despite your purported neutrality—relationships, motivations, and desires you perceived (and perhaps only you could see).

to improve misunderstanding
no. 144

Write a scene in which an event is withheld from the reader.

to (further) improve misunderstanding
no. 145

Write a dialogue between two characters, one of whom cannot hear what the other is saying.

on ambiguity

no. 146

Create a character who sees something no one else does. This thing should be either very large or very small.

picture method
no. 147

On a day or in a moment when you are in a disturbed or distracted state, when you are feeling a feeling you do not wish to feel, try focusing on this state rather than ignoring it or attempting to escape it.

Maybe even put a note on your desk or computer to remind yourself to do this when the time comes.

Make yourself as aware as possible of the mood. Let yourself drift gently into it and note in writing all the fantasies and other associations that come up.

Turn inward. Permit a fantasy image to take form.

Allow it to shift, divide, transform. Follow its movements. Offer it words.

vibrancy

no. 148

Write a "sense portrait" of yourself—a portrait or anatomy of your senses.

Do you have a dominant sense or a sense that is unusually keen, a sense that you think of as a superpower? Was there a time when a sense or senses helped or saved you? Do you have a theory of how your senses are interrelated? What have other people told you about how you (in particular) sense the world? Make notes on any incidents you remember, whether of being told you were too sensitive or not sensitive enough—or, perhaps, of being praised for your sensitivity. Are there senses you consider lesser or weaker in some way? Senses you prefer not to engage with? A sense that obsesses you?

nth sense

no. 149

Write about a time you experienced an uncanny coincidence, intu-ition, premonition, or déjà vu. Pay particular attention to any visions, sounds, feelings, smells, etc. that you associated with this experience.

temporality of touch
no. 150

Make a record of moments when you touched someone or something or were touched in recent memory. Start with the past few days and see how far back you can go. Or write in the other direction, from your earliest memory of touch toward the present. Keep a journal or write an autobiography of touches and sensations.

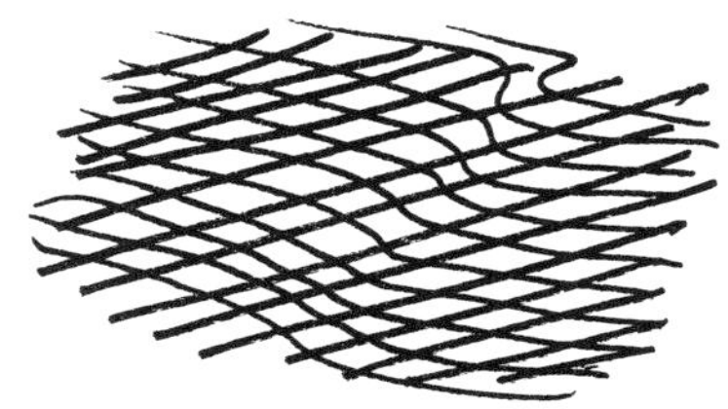

exercise for manifestation
no. 151

Write down what you wish for. Be detailed and honest, even if what you wish for embarrasses you (a little or a lot). For example, if what you wish for is a companion, note the qualities you desire in that companion. (Again, be detailed and honest.) You might even speculate a little about why you desire these qualities.

Look for images that correspond to what you wish for, even if they only depict your wishes indirectly, and keep them close at hand, even if you don't look at them frequently. (Feel free to examine them whenever you like.)

When the things you wish for materialize, consult this document and these images again. Write the story—or autobiography—of your wishes. If you forgot about your wish or wishes during the waiting period, note this, too.

tuning

no. 152

While seated in a location where you can expect not to be disturbed, permit yourself to allow consciousness to move from site to site in your body. Give an account of what your ankles are thinking now. What is your right wrist thinking? What are the thoughts of your stomach? What reflections reside in the palm of your left hand? At the back of your left knee? Travel to various sites in your body for an extended moment or more. If you think you have a soul, attempt to determine its current place of residence, colors, contents, state. Return to the space of your head.

impossibility and the body
no. 153

Write about a time when you experienced extraordinary pain.

Did you anticipate this pain in advance? Do you believe that your memory of this pain is accurate? What was the nature of this pain? Did you have to manage the pain, and did you know how to? Could the pain be managed? Was this pain shared? If not, have others also experienced this pain? Is the pain ongoing? Have you ever spoken about the pain with another person?

ugly feelings
no. 154

Keep a diary of disappointments, errors, misapprehensions, delusions, hatreds, frustrations, exasperations, resentments, rages, fears, miseries, jealousies—essentially, whatever is most unbearable to you about your interactions with other humans.

Try to give as much detail as possible to these negative psychological forms and don't be afraid of including various affects, colors, textures, and what-have-you associated with them (it's OK if this gets weird). Be granular and particularly attentive to moments when you attribute unpleasant or harmful aspects or motivations to others exclusively, as well as when you attribute such qualities to yourself. What sort of substance do these qualities of others have? Of yourself? Are you sure you know to whom they belong? Track their circulation.

Permit surprise and paradox to serve as guides.

psychic bibliography
no. 155

Create a bibliography related to a mood, affect, feeling, desire, wish, passion, obsession, or other personal or interpersonal sensual and/or emotional tendency. This might be a famous concept like embarrassment or apathy, or it might be something rarer or more specific and minor, like a jealousy of people who are more reckless than you. Who claims expertise in this? Has anyone written about this before and, if so, how?

See where this bibliography carries you.

pleasure journal
no. 156

Create a journal of pleasures.

Use this journal as a location to identify and reflect on various forms of enjoyment, satiety, dream, surprise, relief, grace, awe, fun, delight, and so on. Try to identify such states whenever they occur, particularly in minor or unexpected ways.

exercise for cultivation of peripheral vision
no. 157

Identify the subplots in your own life. Be exhaustive.

Are there any repetitions, patterns, mutations among characters, arcs, actions? How do the subplots relate to the "main action"?

Sketch out these (relatively) minor plots. Create lists of actors within them. Write about something you observe.

story of my life
no. 158

You will need a collection of common (or, if of interest, esoteric) nouns to do this exercise.

Write each noun on a separate slip of paper or index card. (I like index cards! Oh, and I should say, this exercise works well in groups, but you could create a deck of cards for personal use.)

To practice:

Sit in a circle (or, if alone, sit with yourself) and have each person draw a card when it's their turn. Each person looks at the word on the card and has ninety seconds to tell the story of their life using the noun in question as an organizing principle, topic, or refrain. Each person only has ninety seconds (and ninety seconds only!), so they must find a connection quickly and run with it, even if they aren't sure where they are going.

word of mouth, part one
no. 159

Invent a rumor about yourself and attempt to send it on its way. When it comes back to you, perhaps altered, write about this experience.

ghost story
no. 160

Complete the following prompts:

1. Location of worst vacation or trip you ever went on

2. Most problematic habit of most problematic acquaintance

3. Childhood fear, yours or someone else's

Now, using the responses you gave to these prompts (fictionalized, if you like), write a one-thousand-word ghost story. The story must include all three elements named above, but you can use them however you like.

When you are done, title the story and give it to a friend as a gift.

word of mouth, part two
no. 161

Obtain a piece of gossip or a suspicion that is circulating in your community (define "community" as you see fit). Write a piece of fiction based on it.

gentle revenge
no. 162

Before writing your next piece, create a "word bank" or come up with qualities of words you permit or forbid for the writing. For example, limit yourself to simple, familiar words: no continental philosophy, no concepts, no rare words like *micturate*, no lost things like *antimacassars*. Or you could write using only the most arcane language you can find.

Once you have set up your supply of words or rules for choosing words, set up a series of rules about subject matter. Try to go against your impulses and inclinations. If you like to write about visual art and complex bureaucracies, decide to write about an animal. If you like to write about love, write about class. If you're afraid of technology, write a piece narrated by AI, and so on.

To make this (gently) a work of revenge (and parody!), choose your diction and subject matter based on gratuitous criticism you may have received in the past, whether from a teacher, stranger, relative, frenemy. Try to live up to the critic's outlandish demands. For once be "easy" or "complex" or "relevant" or "original," or whatever you should have been to escape the critic's scorn. Really go for it.

When you are done with the piece, read it aloud to someone you love. If it seems appropriate, destroy the document together afterward and celebrate.

exercise for obsession
no. 163

Write a piece that indulges in an excess of description and pointless (although is anything really pointless?) detail.

Invert hierarchies. Spend many hundreds of words describing a door-knob, two sentences on a love affair.

distraction
no. 164

Choose a number between twenty and one hundred. Now write a story in which you count to that number from one.

Try to do this without resorting to tactics like "The elevator climbed higher and higher, from the 14th floor to the 15th, the 16th, 17th, 18th, etc." Rather, attempt to hide your counting, if you can.

For example: "One day, she got up at 2:34 in the morning. Five hours later, she was asking herself what kind of person sics a robot attack dog on a rollerblader minding her own business at half past seven. 'He almost ate me!' she wanted to exclaim."

(Sorry/not sorry.)

Avoid terrible puns if possible and, when you are done, title your story. Then, take a break for the rest of the day.

forty words

no. 165

Contemplate a painful event in your life. This could be something you've long wanted to write about yet struggled to return to or something you don't want to write about at all. (To do this exercise you won't exactly need to write about the event, if that makes sense.)

While thinking about the event, make a list of forty words. These words can correspond directly to aspects of the event, but they don't have to. You can associate freely, if you like.

Ponder this list. Edit it. Think of it as a constellation or matrix. Use it as a resource.

Select five images from your computer. These should be relatively random images—one can be a photo you took, but most of them should be images you've pulled from the internet at one time or another. Hunt around in various folders and try to select the images without too much forethought. Now arrange the images in a sequence.

Compose a story or other brief narrative based on what you see here.

exercise for recovery of joy
no. 167

Draw up a list of mistakes, large and small, that you have made across the duration of your life. Try to write about each mistake in a careful and exhaustive way. Give them names, if you like. This may take a while. It's OK if the mistakes start to resemble one another and you must start over, describing a single mistake, or if each mistake fragments into multiples. Gather them as best you can.

When you are done with your list, you won't be able to go back in time. Sorry about that.

But you can save your list as a resource, write about one or more of the mistakes, give them to a character to hold for you while you do something else, bury the list, drown it, or set it on fire. You could share it with a trusted friend.

what learns?

no. 168

Write a philosophy of learning. This could be your own philosophy or someone else's. What is a teacher? What is a student? Is there such a thing as a classroom? Are there things that cannot be taught?

If you don't consider yourself either a teacher or a student, or don't have much truck with pedagogy in general, write some sentences of unfiltered wisdom instead.

fold twice

no. 169

Source a rectangular sheet of paper. Letter size will work well, if you have a sheet handy. Legal size is great, too. First hold the paper horizontally and fold it evenly in thirds. Open the paper again. You should have three equal (vertical) lengths between two folds.

Now fold each of the two outer lengths in half so that they are half as wide as the center. If you fold the newly narrowed outer lengths in, they should cover the central panel like two curtains or a pair of accordion doors. (I imagine this might be hard to visualize, but part of the fun is figuring it out.)

You now have a folded piece of paper with a "double exterior gate" and an interior space.

Open the paper again to reveal the central (unfolded) interior panel. Write or draw a description of whatever you consider to be your true self or experience. The space in which you are writing or drawing this description of a true self and/or experience is framed by two folding "doors" or "curtains." Close the doors/curtains again, and across this space write or draw the face you show to the world.

Open the paper once more. In the two blank spaces that remain, write or illustrate the ways in which your "true self" is connected to your "face"—if they communicate or such connections exist. Which pathways, tools, gestures, and so on facilitate this connection, if they do?

Use what you discover here as the basis for additional writing.

you'll be my mirror
no. 170

Create a character who knows you. This character might resemble a real person. Primarily, however, they should be fictional. Have this character gossip about you, say things about you that you might not like to hear or resist believing, put you on trial, critique you, analyze you, idolize you, envy you, fear you, fall in love with you. Permit them to assume many other orientations and roles besides.

consent

no. 171

Imagine a character as a circle. This is to say that the character has an interior (inside the circle) and an exterior (outside the circle).

On a large piece of paper, draw three circles, each about the size of a tennis ball.

Label the first circle, WHAT THE CHARACTER BELIEVES, KNOWS, AND MAYBE FEARS. Label the second circle, WHAT SOMEONE TELLS THE CHARACTER IS TRUE. Label the third circle, WHAT IS ACTUALLY THE CASE.

Now begin filling the worlds/spaces of each of these circles with various terms. You could start with WHAT IS ACTUALLY THE CASE if you aren't sure what the character knows, particularly regarding themselves. Inside the circle is what is inside the character—their (actual) thoughts and feelings. What is outside the circle is what is outside the character, which is to say, what is in the exterior world, in a more or less objective sense.

When you come to the other two circles, you won't be able to depend on objectivity, per se. Here, you will need to work with feelings and realities as they are portrayed by the character to themselves and by others to the character. A significant question: Is the character honest with themselves? Also: How do those who surround the character respond to the character's awareness—or lack of awareness—of what is the case?

bartleby

no. 172

Describe a character in terms of a list of things they absolutely will not do.

on temptation

no. 173

Describe a character in terms of a list of things they want to do and are afraid they will do.

self-assessment

no. 174

The "self-assessment test" is a dialogic, descriptive form that appears variously. Tests of this kind may include phrases like "On a scale of one to ten . . . ," "When I think about X, I feel Y," or "In the past week, I have done X Y-number of times."

Identify (whether by yourself or in a group) self-assessments you've encountered. (If you like, contemplate what may undergird these tests: values, assumptions about who is responding, etc.)

Use a found test as the basis for a new piece of writing, a poem or fiction. Alter the test. Interrogate and/or distort or reimagine or haunt it. Fictionalize it. Create a character who runs through it, flitting in and out of sight. Transcend it.

exercise for escapists
no. 175

Choose a topic.

Now write a very short essay or poem about a very short essay or poem you *will* write on this topic.

Explain what the very short essay or poem on the topic will be about, what it will consist of—name the chapters and styles you will employ, words and metaphors, subject matter, arguments, interpretations the reader will certainly arrive at, and so on. Use the space of the very short essay or poem to exhaustively detail the very short essay or poem you will write on the topic.

Whatever you do, do not actually write the very short essay or poem on the topic. Write only the very short essay or poem on the very short essay or poem on the topic.

recalibration

no. 176

Write a detailed description of the audience you believe you are writing for. If this audience is "me, myself, and I," that is just fine.

who is writing this book?
no. 177

Answer the following question, regarding something (story, poem, novel, essay) you have written, from multiple points of view—the protagonist's, the narrator's, and your own:

Who is writing this ________(story, poem, novel, essay)?

Does the protagonist know they are in a piece of writing, for example? How does the narrator feel about the task/role of being the narrator? From your own point of view, which part or parts of you have created this work?

When you are done, set your responses aside for a little while. Come back to them on another day and use them as the basis for a revision of the (story, poem, novel, essay) in question.

drawer method
no. 178

This is a method for "workshopping" my own work that I have found extremely effective.

Write something, print it out, put it in a drawer, forget about it.

A week, a month, several months, a year, or years later—whenever you're pretty sure you'll have become a different person—look again.

volley

no. 179

Some people may be familiar with the (slightly annoying) parlor game Verbal Tennis. It is, I think, a little less annoying when you play it alone and in writing. Here is how:

Begin by writing a question that might be spoken aloud, such as, "Hey, what are you doing with that guy's umbrella?" Follow this up with another question, one that a second speaker might offer in response. For example, "Why don't you ask the salamander that?" Then follow this piece of dialogue up with a response from the original speaker, also in question form. For example, "How am I supposed to do that while she's driving this conversion van at ninety miles an hour?" Have the second speaker counter, "Are you implying that I am not aware of our current predicament?" And so on.

One rule: Total non sequiturs are not permitted. The questions must follow one another in some loosely logical way, even if the logic is absurd.

Keep this up for as long as you can. Note that questions like "Why are you asking me that?" may be less useful in this context than questions that serve to explore and illuminate the virtual world in which the conversation takes place.

When you have exhausted your mind or the conversation, whichever happens first, begin writing about one or more of the speakers. Who are they? What is at stake for them at this moment? Compose a portrait or portraits and see where this takes you.

the double
no. 180

Start out with dialogue: Double a character and have them hold a conversation with themselves.

> Joe: Hello.
> Also Joe: Hi there.
> Joe: You look great.

Next, introduce a conflict.

> Also Joe: Are you being sarcastic?! What gives?
> Joe: I'm sorry???

Attempt to resolve the conflict, using the affordances of fiction.

Consider the following relationships:

> $X = X$
> *X is X.*

What is the space between them?

flatland

no. 181

Compose a conversation with a person who lives in an alternative epistemological reality.

Such a person might be incapable of lying or using language to describe anything that is the case; incapable of understanding the very concept "to lie"; only able to speak in contradictions, paradoxes, or hyperboles, etc.

Invite this person into your world or journey into theirs. See how long you can keep the dialogue going.

via negativa

no. 182

What happens when something hasn't happened or will never happen?

I wasn't about to win the day, so . . .

It was not very scary when . . .

Not reading anything felt like . . .

Nothing felt like . . .

The president didn't like . . .

They don't remember that . . .

Write a single, incomplete sentence with a negated verb (like the ones above) to begin new sentences.

Use this fragment repeatedly, beginning many new sentences (so that the counterfactual fragment becomes a refrain) until you arrive at a new place and a longer composition (poem, essay, story, etc.).

pete and repeat
no. 183

Create a circular work.

loop book

no. 184

Write a story in the form of a Möbius strip. Define this form as you see fit.

myth of symmetry

no. 185

Make use of the analogy form X : Y :: A : B (*X* is to *Y* as *A* is to *B*) in a ridiculous, impossible, and narrative way.

fox and grapes
no. 186

Write a parable or fable.

This piece need not teach a lesson, per se, but it could be interesting to include animals as characters and limit the role psychology plays. One way of engaging with this form is to experiment with the formulation, "When A happens, B is usually the result." Try plugging different scenarios into this sentence and see what occurs. Explore and perhaps surpass the limits of common sense.

agnotology

no. 187

Locate a form of knowledge or practice that has either already been lost or may be about to be lost. Describe it.

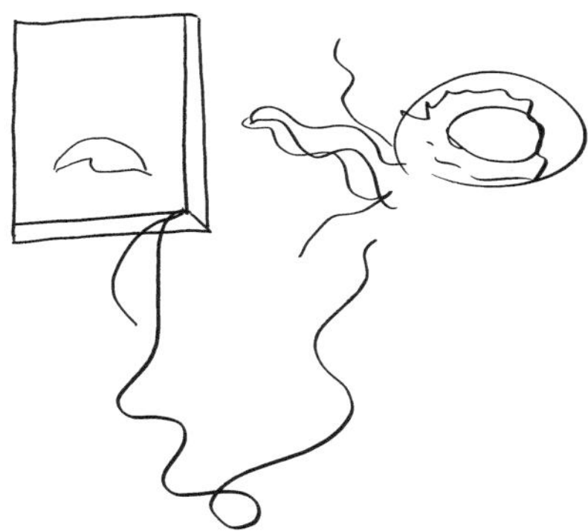

linguistic dead stock
no. 188

Discover unfamiliar diction from another era.

Read period print media or other materials to identify words, figures of speech, syntax, punctuation that have not traveled into the present. (Suggested locations for this research: a library, eBay, your local secondhand store.)

Make a catalog/archive of these materials, then draw from them to create a new piece of writing.

downstream

no. 189

There is a reason why "stream of consciousness" writing is a classic. This said, it is actually quite challenging to write only in full-on stream-of-consciousness mode. Nevertheless, set out to do so. Limit yourself to a single page, at first. Whenever you find yourself deviating from the stream (editorializing, correcting, or trying to think of something to say before writing it—you'll know these deviations when they happen), circle the deviation or mark it in another way. Later transcribe the page, considering the state of your mind at various points. Select some portion of the writing as a germ for something else. Continue this practice until you can fill a page without resisting the flow.

game without objects
no. 190

Invent a participatory game that must be played in the physical world, even if you are the only player.

The game should require no equipment or other materials. Language should be the only material needed, plus space, time, and humans (should you choose to include them).

Write down the rules and describe the course of play.

Play the game.

playing cards
no. 191

Create a deck of cards.

Their number and contents are up to you.

Some ideas for the contents: pieces of language, parts of speech, images cut out from other sources, a daily drawing.

Use this deck to:

— Generate chance-based sequences (for writing)

— Establish the (possible) nature of the past, present, future by asking it questions

— Play a game

Invent a new genre of writing. Give it a name, describe its audience, intent, and occasion(s)—or other aspects related to some purpose— and/or its relevant forms and media.

Now write in it.

pulp fiction
no. 193

Experiment with writing in a commercial genre—romance, espionage thriller, fantasy, or other. Follow the rules, as you understand them. Write an over-the-top scene of heightened action. Use a typewriter to write this scene, if you have one handy. Later, read it aloud.

how to

no. 194

Write a detailed set of instructions for something extremely unimportant, ill-advised, or impossible. Or write a set of instructions for something that does not seem to require instructions. Begin with a title. Then, once you have the title, write your instructions in a narrative style.

Title examples:

> *How to Embarrass Yourself*
>
> *How to Clone Yourself (Safely and in Your Spare Time)*
>
> *How to Like Things*
>
> *What to Know Before Eating a Spoonful of Organic Potting Soil*
>
> *How to Leave*

The possibilities are endless.

Revise to generate a story.

normality
no. 195

Make a list of rules for a place you visit relatively frequently, such as the bathroom, a certain staircase or elevator, your workplace, the deli, a window in your room, a friend's home, an institution, a park, a bar, a neighborhood, a party, a gallery, a classroom, a zoo, your refrigerator, etc.

These rules might be objective. They might be very particular. Some of them might be meaningless or contradictory. They might go unspoken or be ignored. They might say what someone believes must be done, what someone hopes will be done, what someone forbids, what someone secretly causes to happen through the most subtle and barely perceptible forms of control, things that never quite happen but could, what people desire.

Write as many of the rules as you can. Engage in torrents of detail if you like.

Can a list of rules be narrative? Can a list be narrative? Can you transform your list into a story?

introduction to pasta
no. 196

I was once on a bus and a person sitting in the row of seats in front of me was reading a small xeroxed pamphlet titled, "Introduction to Pasta." It was a sunny day and as light flashed in and out of our shared vehicle, I marveled that the world could so abruptly and unexpectedly be made new again. I tried to imagine all the pastas the reader was currently being introduced to. I, too, I realized, wished to be introduced to pasta.

With this anecdote in mind, write and publish a guide to an everyday thing or activity you have some expertise in. Nothing is too small, too obvious, or too well known. Include a bibliography for further reading.

exercise for destruction of boredom
no. 197

Give a friend, acquaintance, or neighbor an unexpected gift. Let the gift be as small and inexpensive as possible (free, if you can swing it). Document what takes place. Begin a diary of gifts you give and receive.

occasion
no. 198

Throw a party of some kind and issue handmade paper invitations that involve folding and printing in some way. The party could be utterly simple—you invite your roommate to drink water with you on the stoop—but the invitation should be very, or relatively, elaborate, all the same. You might even create invitations for no party at all.

Create an audio guide for a familiar place, such as a hallway, room, road, or inside of your shoe. Choose stopping places. Engage histories. Record and offer your guide to others.

radios

no. 200

Go to a public place where many people tend to be present, e.g., a train station or airport, shared transportation, institutional space, a park.

Find a location here where you can sit undisturbed and the acoustics are good.

For an allotted period, transcribe all the language you hear. If people are in motion around you and you hear only portions of what they are saying, so much the better.

Study the words, phrases, and ideas that arrive to you in this way. Save them.

Repeat this process whenever possible.

exercise for habitation
no. 201

This is a versatile exercise, one that may be used both for creating new texts and for revising preexisting descriptions and narratives. If starting from scratch, see how far you can take this act of recollection.

The process:

1. Think of a room, vehicle, item of furniture, backpack, or other relatively intimate container that you no longer possess or have access to.

2. Now consider a compartment or small enclosure inside it—drawer, closet, corner, pocket.

3. Using your memory and/or imagination, make a detailed inventory of the possible contents of this small enclosure. Do your best to make this inventory as accurate as possible, (re)creating the space and feelings it evokes.

4. From your inventory, select one item that seems in some way charged, full, or otherwise significant.

5. Write the "life story" of this item—where it came from, how it came to you and why, what purpose it served, where it went, and what the future holds for it.

Choose the least important location in the room where you are currently seated. When you study this corner or edge or spot, what seems to be located here? If it is empty, how is it empty? If it is full of something, can you describe that? Try to contemplate this extremely insignificant location as a possible setting for an event, the site of an arrival, or a location where someone has hidden something of great importance.

carrier bag
no. 203

Following Ursula K. Le Guin's suggestion in her eponymous essay, write a story about what a certain bag contains, that takes place inside a bag, or which is itself "baggy" in content and form. Write a story in which there are no right angles and no beginnings or endings. Write a story that trembles. Write a story of soft collapse.

materialism

no. 204

Detail a person and create a narrative exclusively through lists of what that person ate and/or things they threw away.

exercise for infinite intervention
no. 205

Take a very short story you've written and remove words to transform it into a Mad-Lib.

Do not fill in the blanks.

translating device
no. 206

Fold a sheet of paper in half vertically.

Now locate a full deck of playing cards. (You could use tarot cards or something else, like printed photographs from a single role of analog film, a set of postcards, a collection of business cards, or any other items you can lay out in a visual arrangement.)

Choose a specific number of cards to work with—it might be nice to use the whole deck or limit the number, if you like. Whatever you decide, write down the names or numbers of all the cards (or other items) on the left side of your paper.

Begin to populate the right side of the paper with a collection of words, lines, or sentences.

The right side of the paper might contain phrases and sentences you yourself use all the time or that you hear regularly. You could collect language in public before doing the exercise, work from your own notebooks, and so on. You could use lines from a piece you are trying to revise or have given up on. You could appropriate material from someone else's work. You might employ sentences or words that describe something you hope will come to pass.

The one necessary condition is that each card name/number on the left should be associated with a sentence or other piece of language on the right.

Now deal yourself cards. Arrange them in a pattern you find meaningful.

Look at your two-column paper key and translate the cards into language. This configuration of language is your poem (and possibly your answer).

(This exercise is kin to procedures used by poets Jackson Mac Low and Hannah Weiner.)

species of spaces
no. 207

Create a simple map. Tell a story within its key.

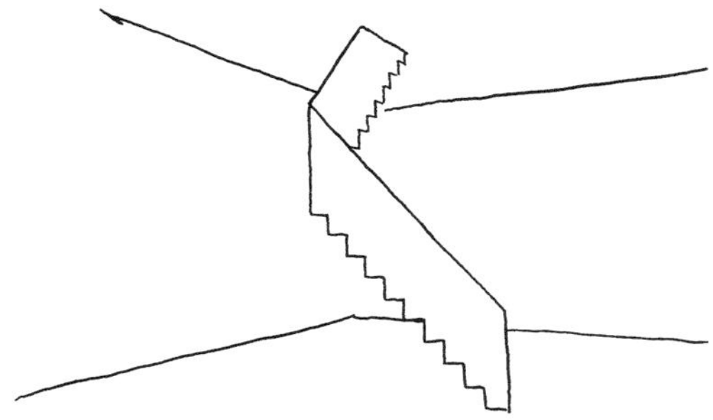

exercises in styles
no. 208

Come up with some styles—which is to say, ways of conceiving of aesthetic value—that have a significant sway, for better or for worse, within the period they appear and/or elsewhere.

Here are a few examples, in no particular temporal order:

— Trad wife

— Interior (spaceship) decor in *2001: A Space Odyssey*

— Point of view of a cat

Really go wild and think of stuff that gives an odd and interesting and contemporary or ancient feeling.

Once you have a list of styles, select something in your house like a vase of wilting flowers or the dishes in your sink and make a series of descriptions, using each of the styles on your list.

Go further with the one that seems most productive.

implausibility
no. 209

Invent a nonexistent artistic movement.

Describe its goals, philosophies, politics, problems, locations, and practitioners.

Now create their writings.

on beauty

no. 210

Imagine a literary reading. You can invent the authors, the poems or prose, the occasion—from scratch. You can write this as a play and perform it. You could stage this as an experiment with others or attend an open mic as someone who doesn't exist. You can make the reading extremely brief or write an account of an event that didn't happen yet was of incredible complexity and significance.

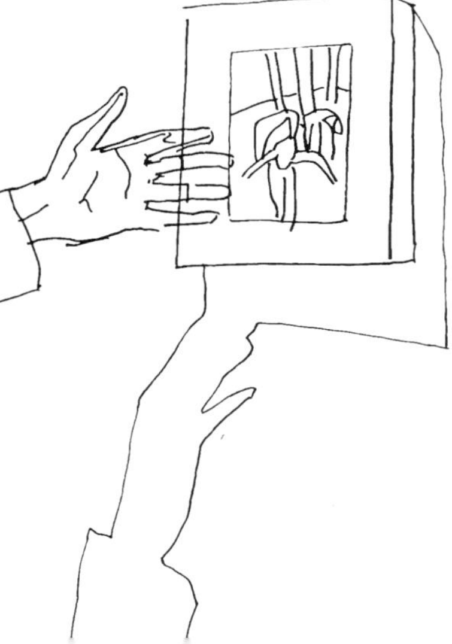

pierre menard
no. 211

Review an imaginary book or profile a fictive author.

heroics
no. 212

Write your definition of a hero. What are the qualities/qualifications, relationships, and functions of the hero? Can someone who was previously not a hero become one? What are the heroics of a lack of heroic qualities? Which hero has no one heard of yet?

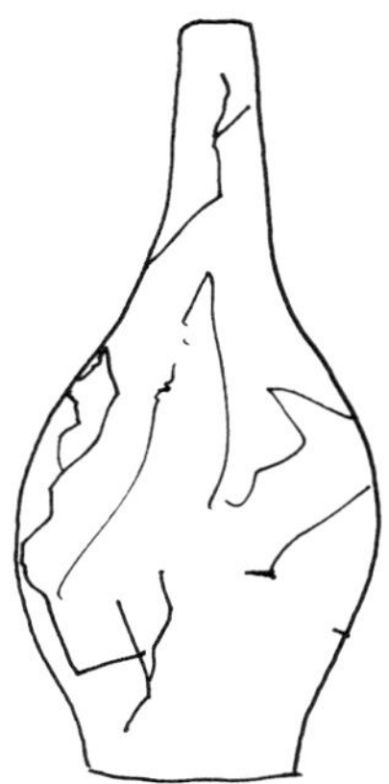

maleficent

no. 213

Write a description of the most malign villain you can imagine, no holds barred. (Bonus: Write about someone who loves them.)

soft study

no. 214

Write a detailed description of a character's garments.

Where did these clothes come from? What are they made of and how are they constructed? How does the way the character dresses correspond (or not) to the era in which they live? Did the character choose their garments? Are they comfortable in what they are wearing? What do they desire to feel while wearing these clothes? What are this character's hopes for how they will be seen?

Alternatively, describe a character only in terms of their desires.

annotated inventory

no. 215

Tell the history of a person through descriptions of a series of photographs or other material evidence that has been gathered or has accrued in a place such as a binder, storage unit, or box. Provide no details about the person other than what is visible or verifiable by means of this material. Consider this an inventory, if you like.

reality effect
no. 216

Make a list of the most irrelevant, minor details you can conceive of, regarding a character.

magick book

no. 217

Write a theory or description of the best possible book (in your opinion/imagination). Does this book already exist? If not, how might it come into being? Which forms, materials, and contents does this book employ? How does it feel, look, smell, taste, sound? How is it arranged, printed, and so on? Who is its author?

reblog

no. 218

Create a print magazine or pamphlet that exclusively republishes material found online.

The more obscure this material, the better.

interview magazine
no. 219

Interview friends, acquaintances, neighbors, and other residents of your community. Publish a serial pamphlet or journal containing these interviews and distribute it in the area where you live. Continue the journal sporadically or regularly, for a short time or for many years.

Create a fashion magazine. Define "fashion" as you see fit, staff your publication with pseudonymous versions of yourself, write about aspects of clothing few people seem to value, and otherwise defy the genre. Invent your own authority to do so. Accept letters to the editor.

mythic being

no. 221

Place an ad in a hyperlocal print publication, one that is distributed for free, if possible. This ad should have no purpose (in contrast to the likely relatively clear purpose of the other ads). Rather, your ad should function in some way as a work of art (how you define this is up to you). Repeat the process.

(If you like, crowdsource the cost of running the ad, offering a copy of the publication in return.)

outside matter

no. 222

Write a piece of fiction in which a story unfolds in the footnotes or other marginal, decentered text (like annotations, Track Changes, a table of contents, index, or bibliography).

Play with various registers of voice, if you like.

indirect mailing
no. 223

Write copy for a nonexistent/imaginary mail-order catalog. Consider the catalog's aesthetics, its audience, what sort(s) of goods it purveys. If it includes images of humans, which people does it depict? Do they smile or stare into the distance? Are animals present? What ways of life and affordances does it offer? Does the catalog sell feelings? If so, which feelings? Are there passages in the catalog in which the catalog describes itself or its mission?

Can the fictional catalog you create play host to narrative, to a story, perhaps one that is counter to its overt goals and message(s)?

A genuine mail-order catalog may stimulate your imagination through its organization, tone, presentation of images, strategies of address, etc. Or it may not.

no. 224

Create directions for a scavenger hunt. Perhaps also create a scavenger hunt in real life, although this is not strictly necessary.

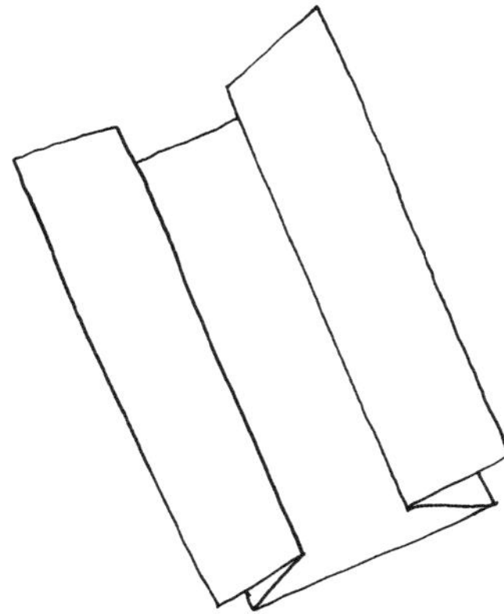

monopoly

no. 225

Write a story in the form of an imaginary board game. Describe what players must do, what they should be wary of, how to win, any rules (either explicit or implicit), characters, architectures, tokens or tools in use, how to cheat, what determines the end of a given game.

site-specific

no. 226

Tell a story by means of institutional, legal, or commercial documents. These might be contracts or end-user agreements. The whole story must take place within such a document.

advent

no. 227

Create a story or other work in the form of an advent calendar. Include: hiding, revelation.

three columns

no. 228

Create three columns on a sheet of paper. Column A is *Actions*, B is *Thoughts*, C is *Things in the World*. Populate these columns.

If you already have a character in mind, you might go through the columns and explore how the character would react to and/or adopt the various contents.

If you do not have a character in mind, select one item from each column (perhaps at random) and form a character based on the interaction(s) of these three variables.

exercise for generation of fate
no. 229

Work with a group or on your own. Come up with a list of generic terms describing movements of narrative. Such terms might include:

> *rising action*
> *falling action*
> *beginning*
> *ending*
> *reversal*
> *crisis*
> *revelation*

And so on. Use language that makes sense to you. Once you have a set of generic terms, come up with specific versions of each one. I might translate the term *crisis* into *lost hat* to make it specific, for example.

If working in a group: One person can be responsible for making one of each of the generic terms specific. Distribute the new specific terms so that everyone in the group has a full set, including the specific term they came up with. Everyone now writes a brief story including all the specified movements of narrative. When everyone is done, read aloud or compare the stories with an eye to how identical plot ingredients lead to very different writing.

If working alone: You will know what to do.

tower

no. 230

Begin a story with a catastrophe, reversal, or loss.

the waves

no. 231

Write a story with a plural narrator.

serial piece
no. 232

Create a series of intertitles. These might take the form of chapter headings, summaries of action ("In which the heroine, etc."), or more standard temporal markers such as "Intermission."

Once you have created an intriguing collection of intertitles, write a story or other work making use of them.

spiral (?) page
no. 233

This prompt was included in a very interesting piece of fiction I read long ago and whose title and author I have since forgotten.

I'm altering it slightly here, in part because I did not understand it as it appeared in the fiction, even as I believed it would be something both intriguing and possible to do.

Write on a blank page. Fine if it's lineated or a grid.

When you change your mind or come to a new thought or find yourself wanting to revise what you have just written, rotate the page ninety degrees.

In this way, you will fill the page in a spiral—at least, according to the piece of fiction I was reading, you will. It does seem to me that other shapes are possible!

Continue writing until you come either to the spiral's center or to another final point in a different pattern.

in praise of digression
no. 234

Write a piece in which we find only digression.

Never get to the point.

vector divination
no. 235

Find a simple but extended linear narrative in a piece of writing. Plan to cut it up. (You can xerox or scan a passage from a book or print out text you find online.) Identify moments of action. Using scissors, cut the text up so that each moment of action is an individual piece. Now glue the pieces into a new order on a fresh surface, permitting the impossible to take place.

Write some prose based on this arrangement, possibly expanding it.

conspiratorial

no. 236

Locate or imagine five unrelated events. Write a brief description of each event (no more than what might fit on an index card).

Now think of each of your written accounts as a description of something that really happened but one that is narrated by an unreliable witness (one for each event, perhaps with varying degrees of veracity). Then, imagine that all five events are interrelated, even if they don't seem to be at first glance.

What larger event do these five accounts of events describe? What information might one or more of the narrators be purposefully withholding? What information might one or more narrators be unable (for whatever reason) to see for themselves? What or who makes these events interrelated? How do space and time participate? Do your best to describe what "really happened," overall.

You will need to use fiction to make this work. Probably a lot of fiction.

beautiful array
no. 237

Write five sentences. The sentences do not need to go together or be thematically related. You can arrange them as a list, numbering them if you like. The only stipulation is that each sentence should be the best, most interesting, most fully realized, most elegant, most mysterious, most vivid, and most complete sentence you can possibly write. Select words and syntax with extreme and joyful care.

If in a group, share and discuss these best sentences.

When you are done, use one of the sentences to begin something new. Save the others.

Sit in a quiet location with your eyes closed. Begin to permit yourself to see images and movements of light and color on the back of your eyelids. *Without opening your eyes*, write down what you perceive.

exercise for immediacy

no. 239

Here is a way to quickly improve a piece of writing. Remove these verbs: *look, see, realize, think.*

Rewrite sentences so that instead of X-character seeing that something is happening, the thing in question simply takes place.

the verb
no. 240

This exercise can be used for revision and composition.

Attend to sentences in which you have used adjectives, adverbs, or both.

Remove these parts of speech. Adjust your verb(s) to encompass or evoke the meaning you've lost during the redaction.

A note that this can be particularly challenging for visual descriptors, but see what you can do. (Such adjustments often generate gorgeous writing.)

the riddle of vision
no. 241

This exercise can be done in a group (or alone*).

The prompt is to describe an object using its visual qualities only. You cannot name it or say what it is used for. You may only write what you can see.

If in a group, each person reads aloud what they've written, and others must guess what the object is. It can be particularly interesting if the objects are located in the same room with the group. Or if the gathering occurs in a public space.

*I've also done this on my own. For fun.

chroma

no. 242

Choose a color. Write in praise of this color or against it. Write a theory of it. Write the color's personal history. How was it born? Is it deceased? Who are its kin?

thermal delight

no. 243

Keep a diary of your experiences of contact with air, light, and water.
Describe your anticipation and the instants leading up to such acts
as walking into a cold lake, turning on the shower, perceiving bright-
ness entering a bedroom, drinking from a glass, walking through a
landscape in which snow is melting, searching for stars, tasting an ice
cube.

condensations
no. 244

This may be an exercise for revision, or it may be something else.

Summarize a longer piece of writing using a single word as follows:

- As a verb

- As a noun

- As an adjective

- As an adverb

Use these condensations as a guide.

miniature

no. 245

Write a piece in which all things described are miniatures. Gaze into a miniature world. Describe what takes place there.

Embed your description within another piece of writing that occurs at a larger scale.

human comedy

no. 246

Tell a riddle, which is to say, a joke that requires some guessing. Write a story that takes the form of a riddle. Or find a very bad joke and use it as the basis of a story. Invent a character who tells such very bad jokes. Ask the character to write the story on your behalf. Intervene before they can finish it.

dad joke
no. 247

Use a pun as the basis for a story or poem.

elusiveness of nonsense
no. 248

Write a piece that makes no sense.

That is all. But check it again to make sure it makes no sense.

And again.

And again.

Because it might just be absurd, not truly nonsensical.

And again.

And again . . .

rorschach

no. 249

Write a single sentence that you like on a thin piece of paper. Turn the paper over. You should be able to see marks (your backward writing). Squint at the marks and interpret them to perceive another sentence. (You'll be forced to be imprecise here.)

For example, a first sentence, *We all know cats are fun*, could produce a second sentence, *Now Jo has wanted his elf.* (What you see may have more to do with your handwriting than the objective words.)

Compose a piece that begins with the first sentence and ends with the second. Or use this translation method in another way.

(If you are familiar with the work of Raymond Roussel, you will know that this procedure comes from him, here lightly altered by me.)

paragraph divination
no. 250

Select a short paragraph from a book or other location. Literary writing works well for this exercise, but you might also choose a paragraph from a scientific paper or another source with field-specific language.

Copy (electronically or longhand) the paragraph onto a new page.

Begin by creating a new version of the paragraph in which you have removed all the adjectives, adverbs, prepositional phrases, and relative clauses (who . . . , that . . . , which . . . , etc.) from the paragraph's sentences.

Now transform any noun in the remaining paragraph to its opposite. This may take some thought, as not all nouns, particularly proper nouns, have opposites. Do your best and don't be put off by absurdity.

Do the same for all verbs.

Read the resulting paragraph aloud. Then summarize it in your own words in just two to three sentences. Your summary may seem ludicrously inconsequential or nonsensical.

Continue, if you like, writing freely, using what strikes you as a point of departure. Allow intuition to take the lead.

These questions may be useful: What are the sentences about? What takes place in them? What interests you about them? What seems important? Who or what has appeared here? Have events, persons, or moods changed? Are things going wrong? Are things going well?

cento

no. 251

Transform a newspaper or magazine to your own ends. Work from print and use scissors and glue. Collage events. Reimagine the roles images play. Allow temporalities to bump up against and contradict one another. Intervene in the chosen outlet daily, monthly, quarterly, etc., depending on its publication schedule.

an image of genre
no. 252

A suggestion for beginning, with genre in mind.

Begin not with a narrative, theme, or character, but with genre itself.

Choose a genre. Consider it a container, landscape, machine, or series of shapes. Which works of writing, for you, epitomize it?

Draw some pictures (define this task as you see fit): of the genre in general, of specific works.

Now write a work that feels intimate to you.

Write a work of weak literature. Let this piece disidentify with its own genre or type. Let it disidentify with literature itself, if you like. Let it crumble and/or fail.

weak spot
no. 254

Return to a certain part of something you've written that you know isn't working.

Don't try to fix it.

Paste this nonworking section into a new document and instead of trying to fix it, expand it. Read it over and try to write even more intensely in its style—or write something new entirely in its style.

Attempt to attend to what you were doing in the nonworking section. How can you try to do this (much) more or do only this?

live redaction

no. 255

Instead of writing in the voice of a narrator, your own voice, or the voice of a character, write in the voice of an editor.

For example, the sentence "The cat is excellent" could be rendered:

Please choose a more exciting animal than "cat" and a more specific adjective than "excellent."

Or:

You can write, "The cat is excellent," but erase the word cat *and replace it with* feline.

Or other permutations, according to the goals and preferences of the editor.

See how long you can keep this going.

[frame]

no. 256

Don't write the piece.

Write about all the conditions and reasons for writing the piece. Write about what will happen after you write the piece, why it's necessary to write it, the personal experiences that have brought you to this point, and so on.

endless andness

no. 257

Write a short story of one thousand words or less. Now remove all the hard stops—all the periods and capitalized beginnings of new sentences. Replace this punctuation, etc. with the conjunction *and*.

Select a poem. Recopy the text (by hand or by typing) so that there are no longer stanzas, line breaks, or lineation of any kind. (Basically, you are making the poem into a block of nonstandard prose.) Retain the original punctuation and capitalization, even if this makes for incorrect, incomplete, or run-on sentences. Set this piece of text aside for a few days.

Once you are pretty sure you have forgotten the original lineation of the poem, return to your prose block and re-lineate it. You can try to recreate the original poem or fashion something new. Make several versions.

When you are done, compare your work to the original. Do you perceive losses? Gains?

This exercise is very interesting when undertaken using a famous poem, especially with a group of people who believe they know the poem in question quite well. (A line break is a sort of absence, and we seem not to perceive or recall absence with much accuracy, as humans.)

microscript

no. 259

Wait to receive a piece of paper that is a scrap. The paper must turn up in a pocket or have been left on a desk or table or in a drawer. It must be a fragment and have become disconnected from the narrative of your life in some way. It might also be a found item, with no direct connection to your own experience save that you chose to pick it up.

Your task, should you choose to accept it, is to write a (very) short story on this scrap. The story must have a beginning, middle, and end. You must also find a way to mention or thematize the scrap itself within the story. Again, the words of your story must fit on the scrap.

Consider writing a collection of such stories.

refrain
no. 260

Use a song to structure a story.

active reading

no. 261

Instead of engaging in literary analysis, develop a performance as an interpretive strategy for something you are reading.

Treat a poem or paragraph as a score, source of dramatic dialogue, or other. Include movement and/or blocking. Create a makeshift costume. Set the page to music if you feel so inclined.

This can also be used as an alternative mode of "workshop" or means of generating unforeseen experience in the classroom.

rebus

no. 262

Write a piece that serves as a series of instructions for how to read an imaginary text or how to look at imaginary pictures.

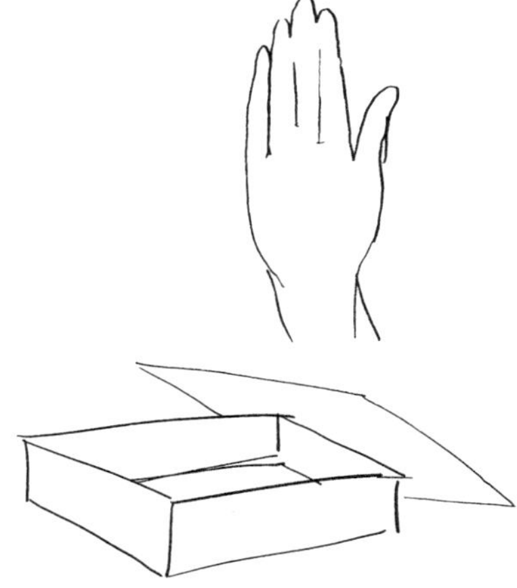

false friends

no. 263

Write a false etymology. Be elaborate, untrue, convincing.

meme logic
no. 264

Create a fictional language. Perhaps it is, in some way, impossible.

Who speaks and who writes it, if anyone does? Describe and/or depict
the writing system, if one exists.

lunar origins of the alphabet
no. 265

The title of this exercise comes from an essay-poem by Giovanna Sandri. Sandri describes the history of a mystical alphabet that preceded the Phoenician system (the alphabet from which the Greek and, eventually, Italic alphabets derive). The letters of this mystical alphabet were composed of cuttings from fragrant trees; here sense and linguistic difference were olfactory and kinetic in nature as well as inscribed and visible.

One implication of Sandri's account is that there may exist unacknowledged, unnamed, forgotten, or excluded forms of language and communication.

Hsuan L. Hsu writes that olfaction is "a sense fraught with uncertainty and ambiguity insofar as it blends representational and material modes of communication."

The exercise: Identify a scent, smell, fragrance, odor, reek, whiff, bouquet. Follow it through time and space—especially time. Consider it a signal and a form of language. Is it a manufactured scent? An organic one? What does it express or convey?

Write a short scene, essay, or other in which olfaction is treated as the primary sense. Or narrate the new history you have learned in another way.

mixed signals
no. 266

Write something that cannot be read. It's OK if it can be read partially or is recognizable as language, but it should not be legible in full or primarily legible.

Use redaction, ellipses, unreal letters, too much ink or too little, repetitions, reflections, excesses, lacks, difficult tools, found materials, words and nonwords, pictures, breath, objects, soil, saliva, loss.

Have a character write a (fictional) poem or (fictional) work of fiction. Be sure to title it.

Include the character's poem or work of fiction in a story or other narrative about the character.

the worst

no. 268

Here is a fun game: Write something really and truly terrible. It should be something written in what you believe to be the worst style, with the worst content, for the worst reasons.

Recall that, to be genuinely reprehensible, a piece of writing must be good or attractive in some way. For this reason, you will need to identify what is good about what you think is the worst, so that you can imitate that bad goodness and thereby reveal its awfulness.

No cheating! If the writing you produce isn't any good, it probably isn't bad enough.

house of leaves

no. 269

Make a three-dimensional representation of a piece of writing you are working on.

Treat the representation as a draft. Have fun. Use found materials, such as packaging you might otherwise discard.

It's OK if it falls apart.

walk-through
no. 270

Draw a floor plan of a house, apartment, or other building, real or imagined. Make this plan more or less detailed, depending on your preference, and include doors, windows, furnishings, or other contents.

Now write a story about what takes place here, using the floor plan in some significant way.

glamour of anachronism
no. 271

This is sort of a classic writing exercise, but I think it's no worse for that. If you are in a state of boredom with your own language (or with others'), this might help.

Select for yourself (or your class or whomever) a poem written before the year 1400. Since modern English didn't exist at this time, you'll probably need a translation. It might be nice to have a few different translations. Also, it might be nice to select a poem that isn't in (any) English, at all.

Now acquire a second, very recent text. I wish celebrity magazines were what they used to be—you can probably still find a pretty good one at a supermarket—or get a recent newspaper or other print item that has a lot of language in it. You might be able to use a mail-order catalog, appliance instruction manual, lengthy update on something or other from your health insurance provider, or alumni magazine. Use what you've got.

Create a new translation of the poem using language derived from the contemporary print item. Find all the words you use in the new version (translation) of the poem in the contemporary print item, no exceptions.*

*If you have a lot of time and/or interest, you could also do this with an olde prose work and some contemporary fiction, self-help, or other.

keywords

no. 272

Create a dictionary or a collection of significant words according to a single criterion: a collection of words you most love, words you wish existed, words that have defined your life, words that circulate in a given community, words associated with a transformation you hope to see, among other possibilities.

phenomenology of naming
no. 273

Imagine a moth walking slowly across a windowsill or along the edge of your page.

As it walks, its wings move.

As the moth continues to move in your mind, try to identify a verb in English that aptly describes the motions the moth's wings make against each other as it goes along.

Be attentive to scale and intensity.

Make a list of all the verbs you can come up with and scrutinize them closely. Do they correctly convey the movement of the moth's wings?

(A note that you will eventually have to reject all of your verbs, because no such word exists in the English language, although perhaps it exists in others.)

lipogram
no. 274

Ban a letter from the alphabet. Write a story or poem in spite (or because) of its absence.

glass mountain
no. 275

Write a story in which no time passes.

utopic

no. 276

Write a story in which nothing happens, in which no one appears, in which there is no action, in which there is no description, in which there is no point of view, in which nothing is ever said, that no one ever wrote, and that never ends.

kafka
no. 277

Write the tale of an ambiguous miracle.

multiple choice
no. 278

The forked path or blind choice is familiar to us from labyrinths, enchanted gardens, visual art, and cinema, but its relationship to sentences may be less apparent. Here is an exercise related to mazes, staircases, and possibility that turns the inanity of administrative control into a form of play.

Write a brief narrative in the form of a multiple-choice exam. Describe the previous day's events as a multiple-choice exam. Describe your family as a multiple-choice exam. Describe your lover as a multiple-choice exam. Write a travel narrative that is a multiple-choice exam. Write the history of your country as a multiple-choice exam. Compose a story of a life that is a multiple-choice exam. Or choose another subject for your test.

Complete the exam. Score your results.

zwicky box

no. 279

This method is based on a matrixial tool identified by the Bulgarian Swiss astronomer Fritz Zwicky (who, as it so happened, first theorized dark matter). You can use this method for various things, but let's imagine it as a tool for writing a story.

Across the top of your matrix/spreadsheet write a series of categories, such as *location*, *problem*, *loss*, *people*, *genre*, *weather*, and so on. These are the column titles. Fill each column with various contents. If I'm filling out the "location" column, I might try:

> at home
> on a cloud
> Philadelphia
> Urmia, Iran
> 50 years in the future
> Manhattan in the 1990s
> *And so on.*

After populating all your columns, create a series of different combinations, taking one item from each column to produce a series of qualities for a story (for example, one that takes place in Philadelphia, includes a global health crisis, is about divorce, concerns artists, is written as a picaresque, and features a meteor shower).

Continue to explore combinations until you find one that feels particularly impossible or strange or unexpected or vivid to you.

Write this story.

mentor

no. 280

Write a piece of fiction that takes the form of a letter of recom-
mendation. This letter could be about someone on whose behalf
you'd never be asked to write, whom you dislike, who is not currently
alive, who does not exist, and so on. It could be written by a confused
person, a vengeful person, an unrequited lover, an animal, a celebrity
or historical figure.

joy of cooking

no. 281

Think of something big, social, and at once tangible and intangible. This could be an emotion, an institution, a myth, a practice, or other. This thing could be a real thing, or it might be imaginary. It might be a kind of artwork you make regularly or a genre of writing that is important to you.

Obtain an index card. What you write on it must take the form of a recipe, with ingredients and directions. What you write must also fit on the index card.

Write instructions for creating the thing you selected in the form of a recipe. How is this thing composed? How is it made? What do you need to have and do to make it? Is there anything we need to know about how it should be offered to others?

Use the recipe as the basis for a story, essay, or something else.

more mysteries of scale

no. 282

Write a thirty-page sentence. (If you can do this, you are ready for the big leagues!)

holding pattern
no. 283

Write a message to someone whose work you admire. This person need not be alive, and you need not send the letter.

exercise against caution
(aka "the compliments game"), no. 284

In a group, everyone gets a set of blank index cards—the same number of index cards as there are participants, minus one.

On one side of each card in their set, everyone writes the names of all the other participants (one name per card). On the other side, everyone writes down a quality they admire in the person whose name is on the reverse. (What each person writes will remain anonymous, unless the group chooses otherwise.)

Once everyone is done writing, the cards should be collected and reorganized into sets by name. Each person receives the cards with their name. Allow ample time for reading.

There may be some uncomfortable remarks as well as compliments (crushes, jealousy—all that is here, too), but in my experience the overall tenor is of surprise. You really can't see yourself as others see you.

When everyone is ready, take time to discuss. Someone might want to read from their cards, or it may be interesting to pose questions, e.g., what is the game about, what is it for, what does it bring into being that did not exist previously?

alphabet's ladder
no. 285

In another life, I heard some advice about how to talk to other people in order to seem interesting and nice.

Although "advice about how to talk to other people in order to seem interesting and nice" should probably be taken with a grain of salt, I've always retained this weird instruction. I should be clear that I don't understand how or why anyone would think this would work, but here is the advice, anyhow:

> *When you must talk to someone you don't know for an extended period, use the alphabet as a basis for everything you say. Your first remark should be based on A, your second on B, and so on. For some reason, this will make you seem very interesting and very nice.*

And yet. Could this advice be used as the basis for a dialogue, story, other? How long could you speak in this way before someone noticed? What if the person did not notice? What if you spoke this way forever or otherwise inclined toward letters as a mystical means of arrangement?

Alternatively: Compose a poem, essay, story, or other in the form of an abecedarium, organizing its parts by making use of the letters from A to Z.

travesty

no. 286

Write a parodic version of a work that, in your opinion, has qualities worthy of satire.

fictions of control
no. 287

Compose a series of fictional slogans, truisms, or aphorisms. "X = Y" is one popular format for such things, but feel free to invent your own.

Use these slogans to imagine an ideology, political situation, religion, cosmetics empire, and so on that you describe in a piece of fiction.

invisible exhibition
no. 288

Create a series of wall labels for nonexistent, imagined, or fictional(ized) artworks.

Include such details as title(s), date(s), author(s), materials, provenance, exhibition history, location(s), duration, curator's perspective and/or inferences . . .

Here, to get you started, is a "bank" of potential materials:

. . . plastic sacks of colored sand, acrylics and cans of enamel, unusable brushes, broken pencils, plywood fragments, balls of twine and coils of salvaged wire, sculpting clay, copper mesh, candle wax, bags of blond hair covered with candle wax, gouache and charcoal sticks, faux bois paper, newspaper, pots of black ink, cardboard covered with white paint, tacks, deconstructed leather bindings, boards, cutout endpapers embellished with pasted papers, pasted-on cloth mounted on wood, partially painted wood, painted plaster and cork mounted on canvas but abandoned, a stuffed silk stocking suspended in a wooden frame, several plaster heads with painted cloth, googly eyes, two steel rods, part of a wooden chair hung on a board, a piece of a door covered in bits of laminated hessian cloth, Masonite, oils, unidentifiable plastic objects, a neon tube, a plastic rod, felt, cord, cotton, a dented pail, a sack, dust . . .

paint by numbers, part one

no. 289

1. Select a location. Out-of-doors might be nice, but a window would work, too.

2. From this location, make a linguistic sketch of what you can see. Try to be exhaustive.

3. When you are done, underline or circle all the places where color appears. Make a list of these colors on another part of your page. Compare the list to the landscape. Are there any colors you have missed? Put those here, too.

4. Next, annotate the colors: Which red is that? What sort of black? How do other colors appear within the colors you have identified? Do you know the precise names of the colors?

paint by numbers, part two

no. 290

Take your list of found colors to a paint store or art supply store and begin another set of comparisons. How are colors named in these contexts? Are there color-related words you are not familiar with, histories of the pigments to discover, and so on?

The idea here is to create an archive of colors. It's a research project, in this sense. It may lead to something else.

cloud atlas

no. 291

Sit outside and make a description of the weather. Engage with the luminous grain of atmospheric and thermal detail, identifying particularities of wind, moisture, light, pressure, the rate and momentum of time.

light in utopia
no. 292

Identify an improvement that could be made to a public place you visit frequently and know well. It's OK if it's a very small improvement.

To uncover this possible improvement, you may have to research ways in which the place is used and interview community members. Observe and listen. Keep a written record of what you find. Include friends in the project.

Once you have been able to locate and describe the possible improvement, prepare a report. Perhaps this will function as a short story or poem.

Make the improvement, if feasible. Or leave the improvement in the realm of speculation.

the view

no. 293

Find an image, possibly a photograph, in which distant structures are depicted. Select a building in the far distance. Look into one of the building's windows. Describe what is occurring there.

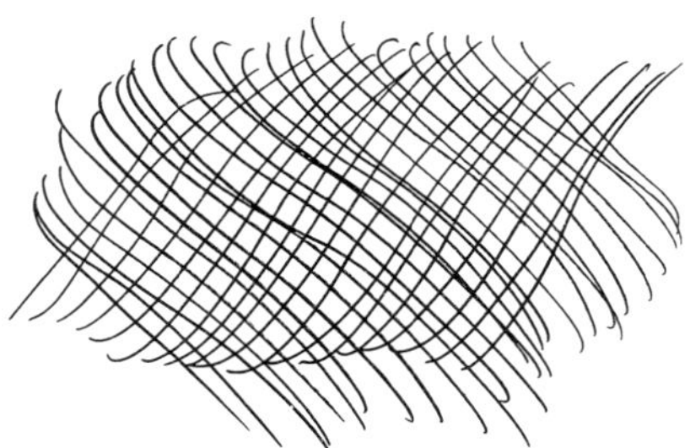

dream work

no. 294

Devise a means to wake yourself up on the cusp of sleep (the surrealist classic is to hold a spoon that you release onto a plate upon losing consciousness) and keep a notebook nearby to record what you experience.

Keep a dream diary.

Describe a character by describing a month of their dreams.

Invent another dream-related form of practice or discipline.

prolepsis
no. 295

Set out to have a vision. In your mind's eye, perceive yourself going to a destination, arriving at the destination, and seeing something significant there (again, in your mind's eye). Now go to the place (however you can), have the vision, write down what you see.

history of invisibles
no. 296

Make a list of some entities that have no immediately perceivable visual form. I don't mean that these should be things whose effects are not visible or whose existence is in question. I just mean that you can't (always or often) see their body or bodies with your (unenhanced) eyes.

Examples: doubt, migraines, orgasm, luck, dust mites, an afternoon that happened four years ago of which I have no memory.

Now write a short history of one of these invisibles. Research it using academic methods and a trip to the library. Or, if you prefer, write an imagined history. NB: The more intangible and minor the entity you have selected, the more interesting it might be to try to find it in an institution's archives.

it-narrative

no. 297

Write a story about the journey of a thing. This thing might be a coin, furnishing, article of clothing, or raw material. Describe how the life of this thing begins, whom or what it encounters, how it travels, if it thinks or loves, how its life ends—if it does.

creature

no. 298

Create a cryptid or monster.

Define the criteria for its creation according to your own inclinations, ethics, aesthetics, and so on.

Locate an unidentified scrap or substance in your home, something that has no use and that you perhaps don't understand and are tempted to throw away. This might be something that was left behind by a previous inhabitant or that fell off or out of something else. (Alternatively, find something of this nature in the outside world.)

Tell a grand story about the magnificence of the mighty acts and significance of this heroic scrap or substance.

paper vehicle
no. 300

Construct a kite or boat, fan or hat, chair or hut, or other useful object using only paper (cardboard counts). Include writing.

exercise for investigation of a past life
no. 301

Find an old notebook you wrote in by hand.

Painstakingly transcribe it using word-processing software.

See where this takes you.

return to the present
no. 302

This exercise plays with memory and attention span, allowing distraction to work in your favor. Begin with the intent to write something. Have an open mind.

Construct sentences as follows (and filling in as you please):

Today at [insert present time], I am ___________________.

Yesterday at [insert present time], I was _____________.

The day before yesterday at [insert present time],
I was _________________________________.

The day before the day before yesterday at [insert
present time], I was ___________________.

The day before the day before the day before yesterday
at [insert present time], I was ___________________.

And so on, for as long as you can.

Try to stay with the task—at least until it becomes totally ridiculous.

Inevitably, you will be boomeranged into another thought (or series of experiences) you cannot ignore. Follow this thought in writing.

log
no. 303

Keep a log of something unremarkable that you tend to engage with each day for a week, a month, a year. This might be a log of what you eat or when, what you wear, what you don't wear, sounds you hear, people you see, or another metric. The more minor this repeat activity or presence, the better. See what emerges.

Write a story that begins with an event at least five hundred years in the past. The story should otherwise be set in the present.

daydream dimensions
no. 305

Write a piece that concerns a kind of space with rules other than those we normally associate with space, as such. The piece might take place on the ceiling, for example, with the ceiling functioning as the world's floor or your neighbor's backyard.

one more inversion
no. 306

Tell a story in which humans are silent but objects speak.

dozen

no. 307

Make a list of twelve ways the world could end. Many apocalypses
might be improbable or unlikely. Some might be gentle. Some might
be unperceived.

on ruins

no. 308

Write about a space that contains multiple—divergent, paradoxical—shapes and densities of time.

counterworlds
no. 309

Begin by choosing one of three options:

1. Dystopia
2. Utopia
3. Negative utopia*

*Utopia written as such for satirical ends, the (insert bright, sarcastic voice) "best of all possible worlds!"

Now imagine a society that falls into the category you have chosen. Respond to the following prompts:

Describe a sport played in this world. Describe a major holiday and a major work of art. Describe a widely used drug. Describe the practice of marriage (if it exists).

Use what you have begun here as the basis for another piece of writing.

florigraphia

no. 310

Find a relatively common plant considered a weed (and not previously known to you) that grows where you live. Learn its name and history.

Take notes on when and where you see it. Develop a running document recording your encounters with it and any messages it may choose to share with you. Ask others what they know of it. Search for people who have tried to learn about, live with, or otherwise cultivate this plant. Explore unknown words, worlds, and beings associated with it. What are its strategies for survival? Why has it been successful? What will its future be?

surrogacy

no. 311

Bring surrogacy into your practice in some way.

Offer to write something for someone else or ask someone else to write for you. Or, if you ask someone to perform a task for you, offer to compensate them or make a trade: You might, for example, edit a letter for them, write a birthday wish, etc.

Another option is to identify something that belongs to you or someone else that is in need of care—a plant, a coat with a torn lining—and devote the time of writing to caring for this thing or being, or taking it to a place where someone can attend to it.

circle or queue
no. 312

Imagine a location and/or event where a small crowd might gather. Examples of such gatherings include: line for bathroom/water fountain, window where food is sold, post office, site at which young bird has fallen out of its nest, and so on.

Describe the people who might be present, their names, and any other qualities you note. How are they connected to one another? Do they share points of connection they themselves don't know about? Will they ever be aware of these sympathies, coincidences, and twists of fate?

pattern recognition
no. 313

Create a social history of an extraordinary class you once took in school (at any time—from kindergarten on).

Interview classmates and the instructor/teacher. Visit the former classroom or other relevant site(s). Gather evidence: reading materials, a syllabus, work you might have made, the work of others. Circulate the history once it's complete.

Fill in the blanks as necessary (students you can't track down, places you can't reach) or imagine all of it. Write the social history despite loss.

life study
no. 314

Invite a friend to become a character in something you are writing. They can play themselves or elect to be someone else—perhaps a lightly altered version of themselves.

Spend time with this friend/character in conversation, on walks, in any other way devised to study the character and produce material for your fiction.

social contract
no. 315

Send a disposable camera in the mail to a group of friends. Each recipient of the camera may take a certain number of photographs before sending the camera on. Eventually, the camera should return to you.

Write a piece based on the pictures, once they are developed.

favorite stranger
no. 316

You can do this exercise as an exchange or propose it as a favor (and perhaps offer a barter):

Ask someone you know to tell you (the short version of) a story about someone they once knew but no longer know.

Now use this story as the basis of your own short story.

When you are finished, show the story to your friend. (If you exchanged stories, exchange the stories you have written.)

crowd as source

no. 317

Create a questionnaire regarding a topic of interest to you. You could also come up with a single question you would like answered. Design a questionnaire with space for responses. Distribute the questionnaire in a public setting or among friends.

Use the answers you receive to generate a piece of writing.

first postcard practice
no. 318

During a daily commute (or other such captive time), write a postcard to a friend. The postcard should detail what is occurring around you.

second postcard practice
no. 319

Write a series of postcards to a friend as you are reading a book.
Each time you read, update your friend about what has taken place.
Conclude the series when you complete the book.

third postcard practice
no. 320

Write a postcard to a friend while watching a film. Begin in medias res. End the postcard when it becomes preferable to continue paying attention to what is happening on the screen (large or small).

chain mail

no. 321

With a group of people or by yourself, create a set of instructions for sending and receiving a package (or large envelope) in the mail. What this package/envelope contains should be collaboratively determined. Let the package travel in a circle among people.

The instructions should contain the following elements:

— Order of recipients, or how recipients should be selected if they are not known at the outset

— Notes about what the package represents or goals for its travel

— Rules for what to add, alter, take away from the package once received

— Any prudent rules about weight and postage

— Deadlines for sending the package on again, once received

— How and when to return the package to the original sender

Once the package has returned to its point of origin (likely you), write an account of its travels or an account of what you experienced while the package was gone.

lunch poems
no. 322

Publish a pamphlet of occasional writing you distribute by mail. The writing should be short enough that someone can read it while eating a sandwich and should concern something in everyday life. Print your pamphlet in an edition of under twenty-five. The production values need not be high.

mystery tour
no. 323

This exercise works well in a place where tours are often given (think museum, historical site, university, etc.), but it could be attempted in other locations. It might be something you do with a group, or you could compose a work of this nature on your own (and deputize yourself as a tour guide).

Create a walking tour of a location. It should include discussion of sites of interest, histories, and, importantly, banter. The tour guide must introduce themselves in some way and justify their pretension to expertise. Lastly, the tour guide's explanation of the place should be largely untrue—on a literal level, at least.

public domain
no. 324

Obtain several paper bags, preferably with handles. (Avoid buying them, if possible.)

Make stencils and spray-paint the bags with poetry or other messages. Give them to friends and/or use them in place of your usual tote or totes until they fall apart.

Keep a record of any conversation a bag inspires.

slow phone
no. 325

Leave (nonthreatening, paper-based) messages somewhere for strangers to find—with a mechanism for reply.

Set up a public message box, if possible.

Enter into dialogue.

Permit anonymity.

Publish the correspondence.

event of speech, part one
no. 326

To consider the eventfulness of speech, recruit a friend. Ask their permission, then record a conversation with them in which you tell them a story. Allow them to interject, pose questions, tell a counter-story.

When you are done, transcribe the recording you made. Use it as the basis for a piece of writing.

event of speech, part two
no. 327

Tell a friend about something you are writing and ask them to collaborate with you on an improvised conversation between two characters.

Record, transcribe, edit. Incorporate the dialogue into what you are working on (or rewrite completely—to your liking).

talking

no. 328

Compose an essay (or other sort of reflective piece) using a digital voice memo application via a smartphone or a handheld recorder.

Write the essay while doing something else such as walking somewhere, driving (be cautious!), going about your day and moving from place to place, washing dishes, folding laundry, drinking coffee with a friend, and so on.

Transcribe the sound file "by hand"—in other words, listening in real time and typing, without using another affordance.

Expand or contract the essay as needed. Consider the meanings of your own silences, as well as the inevitable interruptions.

transit

no. 329

Go for a ride on public transportation with the express purpose of documenting what takes place both around you and in your mind. Take notes, make transcriptions, permit random thoughts and intuitions to become language. Feel and describe.

When you return home, recopy this material and make something new from it.

brief stay
no. 330

Travel to a cemetery and make a piece of writing while you are there.

bibliographic imagination
no. 331

Someone once asked me if I thought a writer should live in the country or the city. I said, "A writer should live near a good library."

One of the ways I begin a project, any project (art catalog essay, short story, whatever) is by creating a bibliography. Often what goes into this bibliography only makes sense to me and it can be hard to title at first, but I find that when I come back to these lists of books and other sources later, they give me a sense of who I was before I began the piece of writing in question (usually, she was a very different person and I need to be reminded of her) and what I did to change myself through the piece.

Exercise: Create a robust bibliography for a work of fiction or poem. Annotate it. Read what's on it. Alter it.

detour as divination
no. 332

Go to a large library and allow yourself to be led by intuition or chance. Read books you would usually ignore. Write something based on what you learn.

all the vermeers

no. 333

Go to a museum, gallery, or other space where people are distracted by art objects (this could alternatively be a department store, a big box store, or a mall).

People-watch in this place. Ignore the artworks and other commodities and focus on humans. Make linguistic sketches of various strangers you see, offering them imaginary lives and problems. Observe. Move quickly.

When you return to your desk, use your notes to develop a (new) character.

metamorphosis
no. 334

Locate an abandoned site somewhere near you; if possible, one you pass on a regular basis.

Learn its history and write about its past.

Reimagine it as a space that was never abandoned or is now newly inhabited again. Write about its future life.

exercise for world-building
no. 335

Convert (expand? renovate?) a well-known poem into a short story
and/or vice versa.

Find an institution near you with a library related to fashion or that displays garments and fabric. (This might be a university, museum, or retailer.) Go to this place and, using materials you find there, begin to study textiles, clothing, furnishings, decor. Don't be dissuaded by the fact that people tend to feminize and trivialize these items. Decide that they are significant. Describe them in writing. Return to this place and continue your studies until you are transformed.

Write an essay about a staircase you use all the time.

opposite day
no. 338

Generate a piece of writing (or method for interacting with other humans) related to the age-old concept of "opposite day."

against the grain, part one
no. 339

Recently, because of a holiday that fell on the day of my class, for several weeks there was a whiteboard with the following informative text left on it for all visitors to the conference room to see:

> *nod = tilting one's head up and down (an expression of agreement)*

Returning to the room after the hiatus, I ran into some students standing around outside the entrance. "You didn't erase the board!" one of them told me. They explained that for the intervening weeks this text about how to nod had been scrupulously preserved as a sort of collective entertainment and joke. (They were all graduate students in a humanities program.)

One of the things the text about how to nod shows is how difficult it is to give effective instructions for executing common gestures. If you tilt your head too quickly or tilt it to the side or tilt it too much, you will do something very different from nodding in assent—so if you don't already know how to nod or have a sense of the basic ground rules for nodding, you are likely to be misunderstood. Even if you have someone experienced in nodding to practice with, it might take some time to execute a nod correctly, reliably, and expressively.

This chicken-and-egg issue where gestures and meaning are concerned will be familiar to anyone who has learned a language or socialized with other humans (anywhere, ever). It is related to the following exercise, which is designed to compel the writer to sacrifice the ease they may be accustomed to when it comes to everyday speech and communication:

Recall a span of a few minutes from the past days when you were in the company of other people and communicating with them. It doesn't need to be more than a few minutes. Describe the exchange(s) that took place without using the common words we employ to name gestures, emotions, and other aspects of social interaction. If someone yawns, for example, you cannot write "yawn" and must instead say something like "silently stretched [their] mouth open, letting out a moan and a puff of air, in an involuntary bodily response to a lack of energy." See how radical you can make your rejection of familiar terms.

against the grain, part two
no. 340

Write a scene in which, instead of explaining what did happen, explain what didn't happen—always in terms of painstaking negation of what did. If people experienced joy, say that they were not miserable. If it rained, say that the sun did not beat down. See how precise you can be, even without access to positive assertions.

last inversion

no. 341

Create a world in which emotions are otherwise: Tragedy provokes joy; kindness inspires rage and is heavily policed; jealousy is upheld as a key to any ethical behavior; there is a "sadness industry"; and so on.

decision tree
no. 342

This exercise may be for beginning. It may be for revision. Certainly, it is for reflection, and possibly it is for conclusion.

Identify a decision that might be a part of a new story or locate a decision in a work of narrative prose, if revising. (This can be particularly interesting in a group.)

Create a quick outline or flow chart of this decision—as a series of options/possibilities, along with the road taken.

Continue to map the story forward and backward from this moment, exploring similar moments of possibility.

Some questions to consider:

- Could, or do, options not taken reappear in other ways in the narrative?

- Are there multiple moments of decision-making (the events, in this sense)? Could, or do, they resemble one another? If so, how?

- Could things be otherwise?

- Could the schema allow multiple possible worlds to co-exist within a single narrative?

excellence

no. 343

Write a story that takes place within a spreadsheet (Excel or other).
Use row and column headers to further the plot.

calling card

no. 344

Design a business card for yourself and have it printed. Engage fiction,
poetry, the notion of address, previous social experiences, aspirations,
annoyances, mysteries of the self, your sense of kindness, and so on.
Use the card at least once, bearing in mind that other people can be
unpredictable.

odd jobs
no. 345

Create a résumé or CV for yourself listing only skills, forms of knowledge/education, experiences, and activities that are either impossible to remunerate or have no apparent value within the current labor market.

For example:

1997–99 Burgundy-Mauve Continuum Enthusiast

Sought deeply saturated red-pink-purple accessories. Successfully dressed in eccentric way most of the time and owned shapeless purse made of shiny mauve yarn. Mastered concept of "total outfit." Demonstrated ability to quietly judge others for conventional sartorial choices. Forged connections with peers with interests in esoteric film.

approval matrix, part one
no. 346

We're often asked to say if we like something or don't like it. Things are either good or bad. Thumbs up or down. Here is a little excursion designed to challenge this practice.

Either by yourself or with a group, obtain a sheet of paper and divide it into four quadrants by drawing a vertical line bisected by a horizontal line. Label the vertical line LIKE at the top and DON'T LIKE at the bottom. Label the horizonal line BAD on the left and GOOD on the right.

(Note that these are just knee-jerk orientations and that you may wish to map different ones in different orders, locations, or continua— or repeat the process, replacing celebrated binary terms with more eccentric concepts such as "SQUISHY" and "NOT SQUISHY." There are many ways to go about this.)

You should now have four sectors:

LIKE & GOOD

LIKE & BAD

DON'T LIKE & GOOD

DON'T LIKE & BAD

Populate these sectors with examples of poems, stories, novels, or other artworks relevant to your thoughts or practice.

approval matrix, part two
no. 347

Using a four-part matrix you have created and populated, select an item from each quadrant and write a defense of your decision to locate it as you have.

two point five stars
no. 348

Write a review of a product one can purchase online. Make your review excessively detailed, personal, and perhaps nonsensical. You might include a reference to history, poetry, or visual art. Post the review, or perhaps don't post it and expand it into a short story instead.

carts crashing

no. 349

Write a story in which a "shopping cart," whether material or virtual, is a central narrative device.

as many lists
no. 350

Sit in a circle at a table with a group. Each person should have a blank sheet of paper and a writing implement. At the top of their paper, each person writes a title for a list. Common list titles include:

To Do
Groceries
Top 10 Albums of All Time
States I Have Visited
ADORABLE ANIMALS
Most Embarrassing Moments
Lost Loves
For Immediate Shredding
 And so on. (Or choose a more unusual title for your list.)

It may be helpful to have a timekeeper who abstains from creating a list.

Now everyone passes their list to their left. Each person will receive a new list. You have ten seconds to add an item to the list before you must pass it to your left again. This process continues for however long and at however fast or slow a rate as the timekeeper and/or participants see fit. It is not necessary to supply items for the list that make perfect sense. Sometimes you may not have enough time to think carefully about what you are writing, and this can be interesting. When the lists have become sufficiently long, they should be read aloud. All entries to the lists are considered anonymous.

in the mood for love
no. 351

Write a story that either begins or concludes with what is sometimes
called "unfinished business."

As a child, I was made to watch a short film from 1973 called *The Fur Coat Club*. It's about two young girls in New York City who give themselves magic-marker manicures, "borrow" their moms' jewelry (including a pin that reads "I'm Coming Apart"), and devise a game in which they must surreptitiously touch the wintertime fur garments of passersby. (This mildly disturbing film is currently easy to find online.)

A proposal for writing: Go to a public place and observe how touch happens. Take detailed notes.

field notes

no. 353

Note a stock phrase that people around you say very frequently, perhaps incorrectly. This could be a meme-like phrase or even an idea that is variously brought into words but used repeatedly (and perhaps in an automatic way).

Make a record when it appears, track it, consider each occurrence a sample or evidence.

Formulate a theory and/or history of the phrase, by means of which you attempt to account for the phrase's origins (of course, it might have no clear origin) and ubiquity. Notice if it disappears. What, if anything, replaces it? How do you use it or relate to it?

word search

no. 354

Create a poem that doubles as a word search game.

The game-poem consists of a list of questions, each of which has a one-word answer, plus a field/matrix of letters.

First write the questions, then, somewhere nearby them, draw a square divided into a grid to accommodate twelve letters down and twelve letters across (or ten by ten, or whatever you like—graph paper might help here). "Hide" the one-word answers in this letter field.

Answers may be written up, down, diagonally, in reverse, or any other way that might challenge the seeking eye.

Your game could be a message for a beloved friend, a warning to your enemies, a menu of mysticism, and on and on . . .

long weekend

no. 355

Describe a visitor and/or visitation. Is the guest (or ghost) welcome?
Will they ever leave?

direct message

no. 356

Design a poetry poster series in which language is the only image. Or make clothing adorned with short phrases or other linguistic patterning. Make a flag or flags.

To reiterate, language must be the only point of interest/content in your creations. No images, please.

Bring your creations into the world. Have conversations with people about your messages.

Write about what you learn; keep a diary of your experiences.

suggestion for ears and legs
no. 357

This might be an exercise for revision. It might have other implications.

Using an online file converter or other text-to-speech affordance, make an MP3 version of a word-processed text you have written.

It's best if this text is almost but not quite done.

Go for a walk and while you are walking listen to the MP3 of your text. Carry a notebook and stop on your walk to make notes on what you hear. Listen to the MP3 at least twice through. Linger and observe things in the world around you while the file plays.

When you have listened to the file at least twice, find a place to sit and make further notes in silence.

Return home and revise the original piece based on what you have heard.

correlation vs. causation
no. 358

Make a list of various events. If you're with a group, events can be sourced from participants.

Now take two events and put them together. Write one version of these two events in which the two events are unrelated and simply occur contiguously in space, time, or both. Write another version of events in which one event causes the other.

In shorthand, this might be something like:

> *I went to the grocery store. Blue hair grew on my sister's hand.*
>
> vs.
>
> *I went to the grocery store. That evening, blue hair grew on my sister's hand due to a strange ingredient I should have known better than to purchase during the day's shopping. I'm still trying to get her to forgive me. She hasn't spoken to me for twenty-eight hours and counting.*

The first passage is narrative. The second passage is narrative and possesses plot.

Experiment. Pull events from a hat. See what happens.

hopscotch

no. 359

Over the course of a chosen day, anytime you hear or see mention of a date/event/time prior to the day currently taking place—whether in conversation or by eavesdropping, engraved in a public place or found in another piece of writing—jot down this date/event/time.

Listen for mentions of historical events, recent and distant, as well as dates and times not mentioned for their historical significance but for other reasons.

If you like, continue the process while online or on social media.

Overall, observe how the past intrudes on the present and take notes.

word clock

no. 360

Write your theory of time. What are the present, the past, and the future, and how are they related? How does time accrue and to what or to whom? Is time a substance? Can humans in fact perceive time?

Draw time, if this helps.

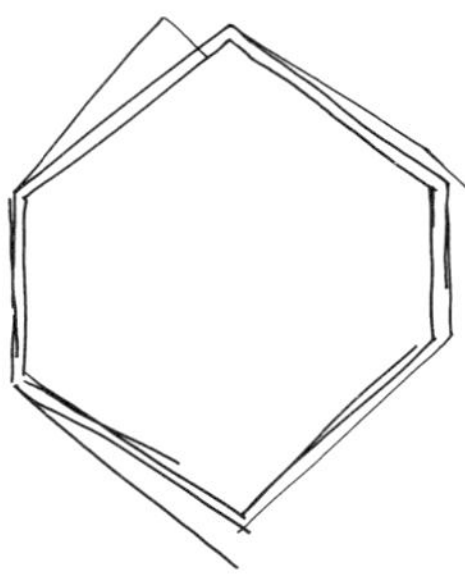

final mysteries of scale
no. 361

Write a one-hundred-word story. Set it aside for three months, then return to it and expand it by roughly 7,900 words.

snail's story

no. 362

Here is an exercise for people who don't have any time to write, as well as for people who do. It is also an exercise for people who want to experiment with writing slowly.

Make a pact with yourself that over the course of a long period—a year, five years—you will write a short story, making very small amounts of progress each day (the "each day" part is very important).

Constraint: You may not write more than twenty words of the story on any given day.

If you write twenty words per day, in one year you can write a 7,000-word story. If you write five words per day, in five years you can write a 9,000-word story.

Decide how long you would like your story to be and how long you would like to work on it, and adjust the words per day (i.e., the snail's step) accordingly.

fate of the senses

no. 363

Compose an index to an imaginary book or to a book that has not yet
been written. This should be a book of great sensitivity, possibly a
book about true things. Think of a title for the book, if this is helpful.

Further: Consier this index as an experiment. You may use it as a tool
to conjure stories. You will draw these stories from bodily memory.
Treat the index as a flawed and inventive companion, as these stories
are not, in truth, fully available. Guessing is essential. Forgetting is a
guide.

apricity

no. 364

Apricity is the warmth of sun in winter.

On the longest night of the year (or thereabouts) sit in the dark and write. Do not attempt to illuminate your room or the page.

Later, transcribe your work on a bright, high-pressure morning.

unforeseen

no. 365

Write a story that is interrupted within the first three sentences. Let it remain incomplete, even as another story progresses.

appendix: a group novel

This exercise is arranged across ten ten parts, with an additional engagement for thinking about ways to publish the writings generated. I've frequently run it as two long sessions. You might meet with a group online or in person; both IRL and remote gatherings work well, which is nice. I believe you need at least seven people, plus a moderator who provides the instructions for the exercises and compiles everyone's writing (sometimes I refer to myself as "the town clerk" when I take this role). The group can get too big if you have more than twenty people, just to say. If the procedures described seem too complex or confusing, please deviate from them and consider the instructions a jumping-off point, merely. The results are very interesting.

a group novel, part one

You can either email these instructions, if working online, or give them in person.

The moderator shares a simple fact sheet with each of the participants, by means of which they will create a character. The fact sheet contains fields as follows (alter them to suit your own proclivities):

Name:
Age (if known):
Description:
Profession:
Likes:
Dislikes:

Participants should fill this out.

a group novel, part two
prep for the first session, continued

If working online: The moderator asks participants to find two images, from any source, which should be as follows:

1. An image related to the present life of the character described in the fact sheet

2. An image related to the character's past (and possibly to a longer, older history preceding the character's existence)

These images need not be overly thought out. The image files should be small enough that they can be emailed easily, or they should be locatable via links if they are too large to be attached to an email.

If working in person: The moderator asks participants to think of two images that satisfy the two qualifications above. Participants write down descriptions of these images on a separate piece of paper from the fact sheet.

a group novel, part three
prep for the first session, concluded

If working online: The moderator asks participants to create a pseudonymous email address (using any service of their choice) that they will have access to during the time of the exercise. This email address should not contain any references to the participants' own names but might be the email address of the character, for example. (It will be fine to delete this email account directly after the exercise is over.)

Participants email the moderator with their completed fact sheets, the two images they have selected, and the pseudonymous email address. (It can be helpful if participants use their personal email addresses to send this information, so the moderator knows who is who. For the rest of the exercise, participants will use the pseudonymous one.) Then the moderator replies to each participant's pseudonymous email with all of the information they need to know to complete the exercise.[1]

If working in person: All information can be written out on loose paper to be anonymously exchanged. The written images can be stowed away for later use.

---

1 The moderator sends each participant the fact sheet and email address associated with someone else's character. (A spreadsheet may help for recording these relationships.) Be careful not to pair people; instead, stagger the exchanges so that each character is writing and responding to different individuals. If you are doing this in person, you can let things happen randomly or try to be more fastidious. Don't worry if things get confused; you can always use fiction to solve administrative problems!

a group novel, part four
the first session

If working online: During the first session, participants will need access to a video conferencing platform, as well as to two email accounts, their personal email, and the pseudonymous email created for the exercise.

The moderator convenes a twenty-minute meeting with participants. Each participant introduces themselves briefly, giving their real identity, then the moderator explains the exercise and presents the first prompt. Subsequent prompts for this session will be given over email.

If working in person: Do much the same as above, but at a table or in a circle of chairs. Read the prompt aloud. Don't have anyone email responses to the prompts. Rather, everyone should write them out by hand on a piece of loose paper and write the name of the character so addressed on the outside of the paper after folding it up. Hand these missives to the moderator, who will come up with a distribution method (I usually have everyone leave their work in a pile and then individuals can come up one by one and search privately for their character's name). Again, no one should reveal their fictional identity.

NB: *Participants should be aware that they will be engaging in asymmetrical communication for Session One, rather than a straightforward dialogic form. In other words, participants will be communicating with two individuals and acting in different roles in each of these channels of communication.*

prompt follows on next page

Prompt 1: Letter of Complaint

Your character lives in a town. They have many neighbors, among whom is the individual whose fact sheet you received before this exercise began. (Use fiction to solve any geographical issues, as per your own or the other character's fact sheet!) As your character, write a letter of complaint to that individual. This letter should be four hundred words or so, if possible, but if it's not possible, that's OK.

You have fifteen minutes to complete this prompt.

If working online: Using your pseudonymous email address, email your letter along with your own fact sheet to the individual whose fact sheet you received before this session, and copy the moderator on this email.

If working in person: Give your letter to the moderator, who will distribute all of the letters to their intended recipients or leave them in a pile from which they can be collected (see previous page).

Once the exchanges take place, the moderator proceeds to the second prompt.

a group novel, part five
the first session, continued

Prompt 2: Response to the Complaint

You yourself/your character have received a letter of complaint, along with a fact sheet describing the individual complaining, at your pseudonymous email address, or directly from the moderator. (Note that this letter is not [and should not be] from the individual you first wrote to!) As your character, compose a response.

You have fifteen minutes to complete this prompt.

Using your pseudonymous email address, email your response back to the complainer, and copy the moderator on this email. (Or give your response to the moderator for distribution, if in person.)

Once the second round of exchanges take place, the moderator proceeds to the third prompt.

Prompt 3: Apology

You yourself/your character have received a response to your first letter of complaint from someone. As your character, compose a letter of apology regarding your original letter of complaint. *Your letter of apology must include a poem.*

You have fifteen minutes to complete this prompt.

Using your pseudonymous email address, email your apology to the individual you had originally complained to, and copy the moderator on this email. (Or give your response to the moderator, if in person.)

The fourth prompt is given after the third round of exchanges.

a group novel, part seven
the first session, concluded

Prompt 4: Apology Accepted

You yourself/your character have received a letter of apology from someone. As your character, compose a response accepting the apology. *Your letter of acceptance must also include a poem.*

Using your pseudonymous email address, email your response back to the complainer, and copy the moderator on this email. (Or give your response to the moderator, if in person.)

You have fifteen minutes to complete this prompt.

Participants reconvene, either virtually or in person. The moderator asks everyone to discuss their experiences during the exercise and select readings from the letter exchanges to share aloud. Before the session ends, the moderator briefly explains the "homework" for the second session.

Shortly after the first session, the moderator will share a document compiling all the letters written during session one, along with the character fact sheets.[2]

---

2 If you are playing the role of the moderator, compile all the fact sheets, exchanged letters, and any other info into a single document. This takes about two hours if the documents are digital, more if you're transcribing handwritten papers. For better or worse, this compilation is essential to the group novel. I promise that it's worth it.

a group novel, part eight
"homework" for the second session

The "homework" assignment for participants is to read the compiled document and use the information it contains to create a visual representation of the town. This representation might be a collage of found photographs, a line drawing, a maplike representation with various annotations, a graph or pie chart—whatever each participant finds most useful and amusing.

If working online: All participants email the moderator their representation before the following meeting. The moderator responds by sharing a random image from the group of images shared by participants in "A Group Novel, Part Two." The moderator can send everyone the same image or share different images with different participants.

If working in person: The moderator asks everyone to bring their representations of the town with them to the following meeting. (If these are digital files, the group will need a way to view them.) Everyone should bring the images they wrote down for "A Group Novel, Part Two" with them to the meeting, as well.

a group novel, part nine
the second session

Participants meet for thirty to forty minutes. They discuss the town they have collaboratively created through fictitious exchanges, as well as each of the visual representations of the town.

What can we say about the interpersonal relationships described here? What can we infer about the town's geography? Its economy? Its history? Anything else we notice? After conversation has been exhausted, the moderator should share the following prompt.

Prompt 5: Time Capsule Discovered

An event has occurred! Today a time capsule is being unearthed from beneath the town's municipal parking lot.

Taking inspiration from the image you've been instructed to use,[3] write a short piece from your character's point of view describing some aspect of their experience attending the opening of the time capsule. The image can conjure a description of an object or memory experienced by your character at the opening. You can write this piece in the first, second, or third person. Email your piece to the moderator.

You have twenty minutes to complete this prompt.

---

3 I like to randomize the second set of images participants shared in the early part of the exercise and redistribute them at this time as inspiration for this prompt. As mentioned in Part Eight, there are various ways to handle this.

If working online: During the second session participants will need access to a video conferencing platform, as well as their personal email account. Participants will no longer need access to the pseudonymous email account they created and may do with it what they see fit.

If working in person: Get together and do much the same as above. When it comes time for participants to respond to the prompt, the moderator asks them to use one of the images they wrote for "A Group Novel, Part Two" as their inspiration. The moderator can be prescriptive about which image to use or allow participants to choose one. Obviously, don't use email to share the results.

After participants have completed the first prompt, the moderator shares the second prompt.

a group novel, part ten
the second session, concluded

Prompt 6: Time Capsule Opened

After attending the opening of the time capsule, your character returns home and, while thinking about the object or place or whatever might be pictured in the image indicated by the moderator, decides to make a change in their life.

What are their thoughts and what is that change? Where might it take them? Write a short piece describing this decision and this change in whatever way you see fit. You can write this piece in the first, second, or third person. Email your piece to the moderator.

You have twenty minutes to complete this prompt.

Participants then reconvene to discuss their experiences during the two writing exercises and to share select readings from their work. The moderator wraps up the session and explains the print-on-demand publication to be produced.

NB: *For the image mentioned here, the moderator has many options— they can select a single image for everyone to use, tell participants to use an image they chose or created themselves, or facilitate an exchange among participants. (If working in person, don't use email to share the results.)*

a group novel, part eleven
print-on-demand afterlife

The moderator gathers, transcribes (if necessary), compiles, and designs a very simple PDF rendition of all the writing created during the exercise, which together forms a "group novel." The moderator may edit the novel and insert any supporting documents, images, or prefaces they see fit. The moderator then uploads the completed PDF to a print-on-demand service and shares the link with participants, who may obtain a print copy of the novel. If anyone prefers that their writing not be included in the novel, this is of course fine. All authors will be credited, unless they prefer to be anonymous.

When the novel is published, the moderator might invite participants (and friends) to a party celebrating the novel's appearance, where participants might give readings, if they so wish.

index

Numbers refer to the prompt number ("no."). A sequential list of prompt titles follows.

A

abecedarium, 22, 136, 285

absurdity, 2, 75, 179, 180, 181, 182, 183, 185, 194, 248, 250, 256, 277

action, 37, 86, 101, 109, 143, 157, 193, 228, 229, 232, 235, 276, 282, 339, 340

affect, 20, 22, 35, 43, 72, 124, 130, 147, 149, 154, 155, 171, 208, 223, 341

alphabet, 22, 136, 265, 274, 285

anatomy, 59, 74, 88, 102, 148, 152, 153

animal, 7, 60, 128, 162, 186, 223, 255, 273, 277, 280, 296, 298, 350, 362

antagonist, 31, 40, 61, 162, 179, 180, 213.
See also character; enemy; friend

architecture, 8, 9, 104, 116, 245, 269, 270, 282, 292, 293, 308, 334, 335, 337.
See also room

archive, 76, 77, 81, 97, 98, 106, 115, 134, 135, 136, 150, 165, 167, 188, 215, 290, 291, 296, 331, 332, 336.
See also research

artifice, 23, 24, 49, 98, 103, 111, 119, 214, 288, 336

audience, 36, 89, 144, 145, 176, 177, 220, 221.
See also reader; reading

automatic writing, 90, 142, 189, 329

autofiction, 2, 4, 18, 20, 22, 23, 38, 41, 45, 67, 81, 90, 113, 115, 118, 119, 123, 125, 136, 142, 147, 148, 150, 151, 154, 157, 159, 167, 169, 170, 174, 344, 345.

See also self-portrait

autotheory, 45, 46, 74, 81, 118, 120, 128, 129, 130, 132, 133, 136, 138, 139, 142, 148, 150, 153, 153, 154, 157, 167, 169, 174, 177, 281, 328, 331, 363

B

backward, 15, 55, 71, 78, 79, 249, 342

beauty, 98, 133, 210, 237, 238, 240, 242, 243, 291

beginning, 13, 14, 56, 62, 108, 141, 182, 229, 230, 252, 304, 342, 351.
See also inspiration

bibliography, 118, 155, 196, 222, 331, 332

body, 88, 101, 119, 126, 127, 128, 152, 153, 243, 296.
See also sensorium; vulnerability

book arts, 87, 107, 115, 169, 184, 198, 206, 217, 218, 235, 251, 259, 300, 301, 318, 319, 320, 324, 325, 363

box, 51, 215, 279, 325, 346, 347, 354

C

calendar, 10, 125, 137, 227, 359

card, 103, 158, 191, 206, 236, 281, 284, 318, 319, 320, 344.

vividness, 98, 103, 104, 237, 239, 240, 243,
    262, 273, 289, 290, 291
vision, 64, 103, 112, 124, 143, 146, 147, 149,
    238, 241, 242, 245, 262, 289, 295, 364
voice, 49, 199, 222, 255
vulnerability, 105, 148, 154, 173, 203, 204,
    243, 253, 254, 273, 284, 311

W

walking, 1, 10, 63, 110, 243, 323, 328, 357
weakness, 105, 253, 254
weather, 88, 243, 291, 364
web, 123, 157, 359
weirdness, 2, 58, 88, 154, 180, 181, 194, 208,
    277, 285, 345.
    See also absurdity; vulnerability
wisdom, 44, 139, 168
wish, 121, 151, 155
word count, 52, 56, 99, 100, 109, 141, 160,
    165, 257, 361, 362.
    See also appendix
word, 56, 71, 97, 99, 101, 102, 114, 141, 158, 162,
    165, 188, 200, 205, 237, 239, 240, 244,
    249, 257, 263, 266, 272, 273, 289, 290,
    310, 339, 353
workshop, 178, 239, 240, 244, 261
world-building, 8, 13, 58, 62, 67, 112, 171, 179,
    180, 181, 182, 201, 203, 209, 211, 228,
    231, 236, 245, 264, 279, 287, 299, 305,
    307, 309, 312, 335, 341, 342.
    See also appendix

X

xerox, 5, 235

Y

yearning, 2, 34, 49, 50, 52, 119, 133, 138, 151,
    155, 163, 170, 173, 214, 351
yesterday, 69, 72, 302

Z

zero, 187, 275, 276

list of prompts

about the author

Lucy Ives is a novelist and critic. Her most recent books, both from Graywolf Press, are *Life Is Everywhere: A Novel* and *An Image of My Name Enters America: Essays*, winner of the 2024 Vermont Book Award in Creative Nonfiction. Ives's work has appeared in *Artforum*, *Harper's*, *The New York Times Book Review*, *The Paris Review*, and *Vogue*, among other publications. A recipient of an Andy Warhol Foundation Arts Writers Grant, she has taught at Brown, Cornell, and New York Universities.

Ives previously collaborated with siglio as the editor of *The Saddest Thing Is That I Have Had to Use Words: A Madeline Gins Reader*.

about the artist

Nick Mauss is a multidisciplinary artist working in drawing, dance, performance, ceramics, and other media. He is also a writer. His work has been included in gallery and museum exhibitions worldwide, including solo shows at Kunsthalle Basel, Museum Ludwig, Cologne, and at 303 Gallery and the Whitney Museum of American Art, both in New York City.